THE OFFICIAL STORY OF THE OSMOND FAMILY

by Paul H. Dunn

BOOKCRAFT, INC.

Salt Lake City, Utah

Library of Congress Catalog Card Number: 75-4325
ISBN 0-88494-278-3

7th Printing, 1978

LITHOGRAPHED IN U.S.A. BY
PUBLISHERS PRESS
SALT LAKE CITY, UTAH

Contents

Foreword

This book contains the true story of a remarkable family and group of entertainers. The author has captured the fun and the fascination of show business, along with its more serious moments, as these have made their impact upon this family. There emerges a heart-warming, intensely readable account of the Osmonds' route to success, from the earliest beginnings to current days of multiple gold-record status and international fame.

Recording the route was the easier part. The bigger challenge was to portray the *real* Osmonds. To obtain the material for this, Paul H. Dunn, who already knew the family well, spent untold hours in interviews with them, both in family sessions and in private talks with family members all the way from George down to young Jimmy. The results fully justify the effort, for as a close friend and associate of the family I can assure the reader that their portrayal in this book is completely true to life. The author has caught their warmth, their genuineness, and their zest for life. Best of all, he has woven this all into the Osmond story in an interesting and entertaining style that defies any attempt to put the book down before reaching the last page.

Many readers will already have seen and heard the Osmonds on stage or on television. Many more will want to after reading this book. But beyond any stimulus to enjoy their performing skills, the book will help the reader to know and enjoy the Osmonds. Having had that fine experience myself, I welcome the book for its power to measurably bring that experience to others.

RONALD J. CLARK

Preface

When we see a top-flight entertainer perform, a natural reaction is to wonder how he got to the top. What is the story behind his fame? How well does he wear the trappings of success? Is he the charming, friendly person off stage that he seems to be on stage? What is he really like?

As with other famous personalities of stage and screen, the real story of the Osmonds is a compound of the public reach for success and the private hours at home. With the full cooperation of the Osmond family, and as a result of many hours I have spent in private interviews with them, this book presents their story. It covers not only what they have achieved and are achieving, their life story, but also what they are.

The book is the product of the efforts and encouragement of many people. I express appreciation to the publisher and the printer and their staffs, and to secretaries who typed the manuscript. I am grateful to my wife Jeanne and other members of my family; and special thanks go to my daughter Kellie, who several years ago could see the Osmonds' star rising and who constantly encouraged her dad to tell their true story. My thanks go also to Ron Clark for his help in selecting the pictures. I am particularly indebted to Jim Faulkner and George Bickerstaff for their work in organizing the material and for their creative and editorial writing the book embodies.

Most of all I am grateful to the Osmond family, whom it has been my personal pleasure to know for the past several years. I have seen them perform, and I have many times been in their home. Theirs is truly a remarkable story. I am proud to be able to present it in this book.

PAUL H. DUNN

1   *Fun All the Way*

The Palladium theater could be excused if her attitude was a little blasé. She'd experienced it all scores of times before — the crowds flocking through London's West End into the narrow street outside, the excited cries of fans as an idol arrived at the stage door, the complementary finery of evening gowns and their tuxedoed escorts, the crowd's "oohs" and "aahs" as the royal car arrived, the unhurried movement of its occupants toward the expectant line of performers waiting in the foyer. The old Palladium had patiently borne with those customary preliminaries, but they were over once again and she was now in the process of doing what she did best — hosting a collection of top performers for an evening of first-class entertainment.

At that particular moment the brand of entertainment coming through loud and clear was music — modern music. Riveting attention on center stage were five handsome Americans. These young men had come a long way — from Ogden, Utah, to a Royal Command Performance in London. Watching from the royal box overlooking the stage were Queen Elizabeth and her Consort the Duke of Edinburgh.

In this position the royal pair were able to get the full benefit of the decibel output. As one particularly en-

Singers, dancers, instrumentalists –
and always entertainers

thusiastic number crescendoed yet higher, the Duke leaned solicitously toward the Queen and asked, "Isn't that a bit loud?" She laughed lightly, struck him gently on the knee with her program, and answered, "Oh, get with it! That's today's music."

And today's music it was. In fact these performers were so much "with it" that they would achieve what no other act in the history of music had accomplished. In two consecutive six-month periods they would have five singles simultaneously riding the best-selling charts. In the "Mount Everest" of the recording industry they would receive ten gold records in less than a year — each one a glowing symbol of more than one million sales for that recording.

The rhythm rocked the Palladium as behind the performers a series of vari-colored lights pulsated with the beat. Every seat in the theater was occupied. While by its nature the audience was somewhat less demonstrative than those the group usually faced, heads still bobbed, shoulders moved in rhythm, and feet itched to follow the dance steps the performers executed with precision yet with apparent nonchalance. Surely anyone could easily imitate that bouncy strut. Indeed, they are the most imitated musical group in show business. Yet this choreograph had taken many hours of work and much concentration to perfect. It was timed, practiced, controlled — and tremendously effective.

They were in the last few bars of "Down by the Lazy River," a song which had become an instant best-seller. "I said down, I said down, I said down by the lazy river. . . . Come as you please. . . . Down by the lazy river. . . . One big fam-a-lee." Taken alone, that last phrase had special significance for the singers, for that's exactly what their group was all about. One big family — by modern concepts one big, exceptional family. For as the posters and marquees prominently proclaimed wherever they played, these were the Osmond Brothers — two words with an impact guaranteed to sell out all performances at any theater in virtually any country.

The song ended, and standing side by side the young men bowed deeply in unison. The applause began, swelled in appreciation. "More, more, more!" The group took another deep bow, holding that position for some seconds before moving quickly off stage. Wherever they performed they could usually reckon on five or so encores. Even then the whistles, yells, and screams which followed their exit would last a full five minutes in a vain attempt to bring them back for "one" last song.

Waiting in the wings as always was George Osmond, where his sharp ear had been appraising his sons' harmonies while his body had moved in response to the beat as well as in the deeper empathy evoked by the family effort on stage. There was Olive his wife, relief written all over her face now that another (and very prestigious) performance had been successfully completed. Amid the hustle of scene-shifters and the usual backstage pressures, parents and brothers exchanged hugs of congratulation and satisfaction, then moved toward the dressingroom. There they did a quick critique of their performance, a session punctuated by humorous comments, hearty laughs, and mutual teasing as their normal, relaxed characters took over. Later they would do a deeper analysis under the guidance of Alan, the oldest of the performing Osmonds and the onstage leader.

Now there were greasepaint and perspiration to be removed, and stage clothes to be replaced by something fitting for an event unusual even for the much-traveled Osmonds — another presentation to the Queen, smaller

They stack up no matter how you place them —
(top to bottom) Alan, Wayne, Jay, Merrill, Donny

and less formal than the earlier one in which all the evening's performers had participated. With the theater now practically empty and the hall lights dimmed, the Osmonds left the dressingroom and assembled backstage. Olive Osmond recalls the graciousness of Her Majesty and the relatively lengthy conversation the two women had. Merrill Osmond has reason to remember better the earlier presentation in the foyer.

"We were waiting in line," he recalls, "and the Queen was getting closer to me all the time. She reached the person next to me, then as she turned from him she extended her hand to me. As I raised my hand I moistened my lips with my tongue, and coincidentally at that crucial split-second a news photographer took a picture. The next day the newspaper ran the picture with the caption, 'Merrill Osmond Sticks Out Tongue at Queen.' "

With the presentation behind them, the final "act" of the evening was to get out of the theater, for the street outside was awash with fervent young admirers. The famous in all walks of life have their idolaters, it seems, those who need from them a glimpse, a touch, a remembrance, and as with others before them, these performers had caught the imagination of the younger generation. A limousine was backed up to the stage entrance, and while police linked arms and held back the swarming, anxious teen-agers, the Osmonds were ushered inside, doors were locked, and the driver whisked his charges away to safer climes.

From the vantage point of their adulthood, parents can either offer indulgent smiles or critical words at the way their youth react to the Osmonds. After all, other top-line groups have received similar adulation. But many parents will be quick to perceive the difference in the effect. Youthful fans are prone not only to admire but to emulate. Parents and youth alike observe that notoriously many of the practitioners of modern music, with their drug addiction, their dubious morals, their scruffy appearance, their gurus, their constant but vain search for self-identity — these have offered little enough of worth for anyone to emulate. How do the Osmonds fit into this confused, somewhat unwholesome and often bizarre scene?

They don't. They don't even try to. They don't even want to. Clean-cut, wholesome, well-groomed, balanced, modestly confident, off stage as well as on stage they give the impression of knowing where they are going. Both as performers and as persons they have brought a breath of fresh air to the world of modern music.

Not that they don't recognize the talents of other performers in their field. They express admiration, for instance, for Stevie Wonder and the Carpenters. They like their style, their clean lyrics. But while they readily acknowledge others' musical skills, and in fact always have a sharp eye for ideas and techniques they can adapt to their own act, they are supremely if politely indifferent to any supposed requirement to conform to the extra-curricular image which many of their musical peers have established. In England, one of the top recording stars asked them to come to a party after one of their shows. Later he was informed that they were "milk-drinking Mormons from Utah." He phoned back, apologized, and asked them if they would mind not coming after all because he did not want all his pot-smoking guests to feel uneasy around them.

Some performers might have been at a loss on how to react to this, since the great and near-great of British rock were to be at the party. To the Osmonds it presented no problem. Alan politely thanked the caller for thinking enough of the Osmonds to withdraw the invitation. The caller was surprised by this reply. It piqued his curiosity. Perhaps he had expected the Osmonds to be irritated at having lost the chance to rub elbows with the high priests and priestesses of rock music. He couldn't have known that these performers have never been "in step" in that way.

To the family, their response seems only natural and normal. "I don't want anyone to think our family are 'Goody Two-shoes,' so to speak," says Olive Osmond. "We've certainly made our share of mistakes. But we believe that statement from the Bible — that if parents train a child in the way he should go, when he's older he won't desert that way. Their father and I feel very fortunate that so far all our children have kept their feet on the path." Olive Osmond should know. She was the choreographer for those first important steps in life.

"Ah, well, so what?" the cynic might say. "That kind of stuff doesn't make news." Maybe not, but apparently it makes music, as well as that other commodity that even the cynic secretly respects — success. Could this tangible evidence of the effectiveness of the normal, simpler lifestyle have a modifying effect upon a generation of teen-agers who at all costs will somehow seek to relate to a popular performer?

While many parents may hope so, that hope alone is not the secret of the increasing appeal the Osmonds are making to the adult generation. For years they had carried the young with them, and then came their first engagement in Las Vegas. "We couldn't take the concert format and do it on a Las Vegas stage," explains Alan, "any more than we could do it the other way around. Since this was our first crack at Vegas, we felt it would be a giant step for our future." It was. The Osmonds were "again" to become an instant success as a new phase in their performing life

Awheel or afoot, it's fun all the way

opened up. The adult audience genuinely appreciated their talents and were quick to stand and applaud enthusiastically. It was becoming more and more obvious that their talent extends across many frontiers.

George and Olive have a quick answer to the question, What is the basic factor in the Osmonds' success as entertainers? "Apart from their obvious talents," they reply, "undoubtedly it was our emphasis on the family. Even their talents would not have been so continually developed and encouraged but for this strong family relationship."

"That's true," Wayne chimes in. "Every Friday we had what we called a family night, and it was on those evenings that we actually began to sing separately and together. We just sang for fun, to entertain the family, really. As soon as one of us was big enough to stand there and carry some sort of a tune, he would take part."

"They could all carry a tune quite early," recalls Olive. "In those early days Virl and Tom took part along with the others — and today they too are quite accomplished musically, though of course they haven't been able to make it their career as the others have."

What else besides the Friday evenings together? "Well, it was sort of a total family focus," explains Alan. "I remember once asking if I could have a friend over for the evening. It was gently explained to me that I had been to school that day and had played with my friends at recess time and to and from school. Now it was family time. We each got the message in turn."

Didn't they perhaps resent this a little as they grew up? The answer is unanimous. "No. We were having too much fun." Merrill amplifies this. "When people found out we could sing, we got to sing in church socials. From there it spread to Kiwanis Club, Lions Club, and other places. Eventually we were taking our group to Salt Lake City. On some nights we made sixty dollars — just for singing, the thing we liked to do more than anything else. All along it was just more fun than. . . ."

Still a focused, solid family, still singing, they're still doing what they like to do most of all. And they're still having fun doing it.

"Down in Mobile, down in Mobile, how I love that pretty little girl, down in Mobile." In 1961 the Night Hawks took first place with their rendition of this old standard at the annual international barbershop quartet convention. But Kansas City, Missouri, the site of the songfest, was more interested in four youngsters who participated and whose combined age was less than the age of the youngest member of the winning group. They had captured the hearts of the citizens and were being projected as the 1974 winners. By then they would be old enough, since eighteen was the minimum age to qualify for prizes at the convention and Jay Osmond had just turned six.

The prediction was generous but would turn out to be well short of the fulfillment. By 1974 these four young men would have graduated from the more limited field of barbershop harmony and, along with two other brothers and a sister, would be the toasts of the musical world. They would own over a score of gold records and would be selected as "entertainers of the year."

After Kansas City, it was back to Ogden and the local clubs again. The Kiwanis Club for three shows, with a hot dog and a soft drink in between performances. The Lions Club for two shows, where they would perhaps vary their menu — hamburger and a soft drink. The Order of the Elks Lodge, and the same routine. Occasionally the boys would have a singing engagement in Salt Lake City. It was a busy, even hectic life, but they loved it. One month, December 1961, they performed thirty shows — more than once three shows a day. On top of the performances they had to practice and to learn new songs.

Today the word *Osmonds* conjures up thoughts of varied and multiple talents which earn even from their musical peers the respect due to a first-rate act. But at the end of 1961, outside of Northern Utah and Kansas City, for all that people knew of them "The Osmonds" might as well have been a trampoline act, a high-wire duo, boxing bears, or a Shakespearian company. In those days their fame was centered around a hundred-mile area of the Wasatch front, Utah's rugged mountain spires which extend broadly from Logan on the north to Provo on the south. But 1962 would prove to be the year of decision, the year that would eventually make the difference between small-time local renown and international fame.

In a way Olive's father Tom Davis was responsible for it. He thought so much of the boys' talents that he paid for a tape recording of them to be made and then sent it off to Lawrence Welk in the hope that Mr. Welk would introduce the Osmond boys to the nation on his weekly TV program. After some weeks the tape was returned.

Later in 1961 the family camper came out for a trip to Pasadena, California, where the boys did a barbershop show. While they were there the family met the Lennon Sisters, who were on the Lawrence Welk show. "These girls were such gracious people," the Osmonds recall. "We were delighted to see how natural and normal a life they led, what a happy family they were." In the early and middle sixties one could not pick up a fan magazine with-

out having a picture of the Lennon Sisters (or Jackie Ken-
nedy) smiling back at him. But with all their fame, the
Lennon family always held to their beliefs and never allowed their values to be compromised by shoddy entertainment material, never allowed themselves to be man-
ipulated for gain. These talented girls were interested in
getting the Osmonds before the public, and with their help
an audition appointment was set up with Lawrence Welk.

During this period the Lennon girls were able to
help also in another way. Their uncle secured work for the
boys at the Olympic Boxing Arena in Los Angeles, where
they sang during intermissions. It was only for one night,
but every little bit helped in those days. After two heaving
mounds of flesh and muscle had expended their physical
violence against one another, or after another duo smaller
in bulk had flitted about the square canvas stinging each
other with rapid-fire volleys, into the charged atmosphere
and through the ropes climbed the four Osmond boys,
bringing a calmer type of entertainment. They were received warmly. When the audience had replenished their
destructive juices, the Osmonds surrendered the arena to
others whose main ambition was to reduce their oppo-
nents to horizontal star-watchers.

Came the time for the audition with Lawrence
Welk, and at the appropriate hour the Osmonds were all
seated in his waiting room. After some preliminary banter
with the receptionist there was more waiting, and finally
they were told that Mr. Welk couldn't see them that day.
"Well, when can he see us?" The receptionist didn't know,
and projected the impression that she didn't much care.
The family left with a dejected air.

They went back to the camper, the boys sensing
their parents' concern at this unlooked-for turn of events.
What to do now? "Ah, well," said Olive, "so long as we're

here, let's go and have some fun." Back to the frenzy of the freeway they went and headed south to the fantasy and escape of Disneyland.

To Olive Osmond there is an attraction in uniform appearance, where appropriate — row upon row of bottled peaches in her basement, white bed linen hanging the length of a clothesline, symmetry of hair styles. In those days she frequently dressed her boys alike. On this particular day when they were playing "copycat," George parked in the lot at Disneyland and one by one the boys emerged from the camper, starting with the oldest and progressing in diminishing size — Virl, Tom, Alan, Wayne, Merrill, Jay, then 3½-year-old Donny. Olive finally broke the pattern when she stepped out carrying her twenty-month-old girl.

The family enjoyed two or three hours of the wonder and enchantment of Disneyland and then, sauntering down Main Street, came face to face with a barbershop quartet complete with straw hats, candy-stripe jackets and white shoes. Naturally they stopped to listen. Being themselves dressed in the Osmond "uniform," they attracted the attention of the candy stripers, who asked, "Hey, what do you guys do, sing or something?"

"Yeah, we're a barbershop quartet too," responded Alan.

"Let's hear you sing something," was the invitation. The four youngsters rendered a number a cappella. The candy stripers answered with a song of their own. The Osmonds reciprocated. A large crowd gathered.

After about an hour of this interchange, the candy stripers suggested, "Come on, let's go and see our boss." Tommy Walker, their boss, was responsible for the hiring of the Disneyland entertainers, and he quickly recognized

The sixties
look –
four
on stage
at
Disneyland

The seventies look – five off stage in Utah

the Osmond talents. Thus it came about that in that summer of '62 the budding artists were signed to their first
professional contract, a three-month stint.

All that summer the boys belted out their harmonies
to the Disneyland crowds for some six to eight hours a day,
Monday through Saturday. That much singing was hard
work and made growing boys hungry and thirsty. Quickly
they learned to "sing for their supper," somehow managing to be around the Sunkist orange booth more times a
day than anywhere else and appearing regularly in the
vicinity of any of a number of lunch counters where they
knew their youth and talents would be rewarded. About a
month after they started, Walt Disney, who had grown
very fond of Jay, began to take a personal interest in the
boys. With his critical eye he saw enough raw talent to put
them in three of his TV specials. This association with the
unquestioned giant of entertainment turned out to be a
turning point in the lives of four "well-mannered" boys
from Utah.

The Disneyland contract came to a close, and there
apparently was nothing left for the Osmonds in California.
It was time to return to Utah and home. In their trusty
camper, they wound their way northeastward through the
Mojave Desert, past the neon jungle of Las Vegas (little
dreaming that there they would be the toast of the entertainment world in twelve short years' time), and into the
familiar landscape of Utah. Regardless of how long they
had been gone from the old homestead, that same thrill of
anticipation would always surge through them as they
sighted home and broke into song.

Home again in Ogden, with the boys back in school,
it looked as though the reach for the big-time had failed.
Perhaps they ought to just settle down, let the boys perform occasionally, and forget show business as a profes-

sion. They even wondered whether their friend Tommy Walker had been hinting at this when, in reply to their request that he be the boys' manager, he had said: "I would love to be. I feel that your boys definitely have a future in show business. But I must be honest with you and tell you I have nothing in sight. Why don't you go home, and if anything comes up I'll phone you."

But when the phone call came not long after the return to Utah, it wasn't from Tommy Walker. It was Jay Williams, the father of singer Andy Williams, and he wanted to speak to George. "Mr. Osmond," he began, "I want to talk to you about your sons. I've seen them on a TV special, and I can see they have talent. Their show reminded me so much of my sons, the Williams brothers. Now, my son Andy has a new TV series, and I thought it would be kind of nice to have your boys on Andy's show, to give the public an idea of how he and his brothers got started."

Well, this all sounded fine, but after their recent experiences George and Olive weren't going to get all worked up about it. It could well turn out to be just a one-shot deal anyway, but there could be no harm in trying. They couldn't know at that point what a fine person Jay Williams was, how interested he would become in the boys and in furthering their career, and how good a friend he would turn out to be.

Out came the camper again, and they set course for the land of their former disappointment. In Andy's absence, the boys auditioned for Jay Williams and Andy's brother Don and then went home, returning to Los Angeles again shortly afterwards to audition for Andy himself. Andy liked what he saw, and the boys were lined up to do two TV shows with him.

Barbershop foursome in 1965

At Tom Sawyer's Island in Disneyland

Olive had to stay home with the younger children, but she recalls well the great day when George set off in the station wagon with Alan, Wayne, Merrill, and Jay — the oldest thirteen, Jay only seven. "I'll never forget seeing them off. They had strapped the great big bass fiddle to the top of the car. I found out later that they had a flat tire on the way. But there were bigger problems than that, because when I walked into the bedroom several hours after they had left I discovered that I had forgotten to put the boys' red jackets in the car. I tried to phone them, and when finally I did reach George and told him I'd forgotten the costumes, he said, 'Thanks a lot.' He went out and bought the boys the navy blue blazers they sang the first barbershop show in."

The boys recorded the TV shows as scheduled and arrived back home on Christmas Eve. (That was the Christmas Jay was sure he saw Santa and his reindeer early Christmas morning, silhouetted against the moon.) When the shows were aired, the mail started rolling in from viewers who had been mightily impressed by the boys' performance. So it was that another phone call came from California to the Osmond home, this one from Andy Williams. The offer was a five-year contract.

Here was a dilemma with a capital D. To accept would mean George and Olive selling their thriving business, which had taken years to build, and staking everything on the talents of their offspring and the uncertainties of the world of show business, a world with whose higher reaches of influence they had already suffered some disenchantment. There were voices coming from both directions. Jay Williams was saying, "George, you've got some good talent there that you ought to share with the world. We'll do everything we can to make life pleasant for you here." (And he did, George recalls.) But family and friends

at home were cautioning: "Sure, they're good little singers, but don't bank on them making any money; and especially don't give up a good business for such a risky venture."

The decision was a tough one. Faced with it, George
and Olive sought the answer in the only way they could
rely on — they got on their knees and petitioned the Lord
for guidance. Shortly they had their answer, and George
proceeded to sell their Ogden home and their business,
retaining only their small farm at Huntsville, near Ogden.

George and Olive had committed themselves to
something more than a great adventure. They were bank-
ing on the eager but undeveloped talents of four boys aged
seven to thirteen. While this undertaking certainly would
not rank in terms of sacrifice with the struggle and suffer-
ings of their pioneer forebears, over the next several years
they would wrestle with uncertainty and a reassessment of
their ultimate goals. Why did they do it? George and Olive
are by no means "stage parents." They would not have
allowed their boys to be coerced or charmed into something they didn't like or that was not good for them. But
they had a genuine conviction that their boys had enough
natural talent to carry them beyond the confines of their
own "stomping grounds" and into the national limelight.
More than that, they had an inner desire to keep the family
unit strong and solid, and what better way to do that than
to be working together?

Off to the city of Los Angeles. The city had been
misnamed. No angel would be caught in the evening traffic dash which greeted the folk from the slower world of
Utah. The freeways of Los Angeles are a monument to
man's urge to get there "fustest with the leastest." Extended driving on the massive concrete in Los Angeles
County deprives a man of his normal coloring along the

knuckles, reduces the elasticity of the lips, lines crowsfeet around tortured eyeballs, and generates more stomach acids than the Angelenos' forefathers, deprived of the advantages of the freeway follies, found use for in a lifetime.

Soon the family was once more in the land where the sun is filtered by the products of self-destructive talents. But for all its filtering the sun falls there in warm soft rays that gave no inkling of some of the cold, hard facts the Osmonds would face in entering the big league.

The contract with Andy was for a five-year period and for a substantial five-figure sum annually. It looked great on paper, but by the time various individuals had taken their cut there wasn't enough left to live on. There was a manager's fee, an agent's fee, choreography lessons, a tutor for the boys, professional help with arrangements, costumes. "If it hadn't been for the nest egg Olive and I had laid away, we'd never have made it through those first few years," says George. Where established entertainers are given everything from expensive hairpieces to chauffeured limousine service, these neophytes were left to fend for themselves.

Most important, to sustain and build their act the boys had to have professional help and training. "Finally I decided that if they were not going to give us any professional help, I'd hire it myself." It was an expense George really couldn't afford, but it paid off. The act acquired polish.

Five-figure contract or not, they got paid only for performances, and since Andy's show did not use the boys regularly they spent a lot of time working up new routines. They were constantly seeking ways to stimulate the viewers' interest. Everything they came up with Andy used — even a routine on ice skates. "None of us had ever skated before," recalls Merrill, "so when it came time to stand up on those skates we couldn't understand why there wasn't one large skate for another part of our body, since we spent more time on that area that we did in the vertical position." They had exactly one week to learn in — and none of them had ever skated before. They bought some ice skates, hired a professional teacher, then camped out at the skating rink. Hour after hour they labored, ignoring blisters, sore muscles, and just plain fatigue. Eventually the wobbly ankles strengthened, the erratic jerking of arms and body smoothed out, the short, mincing steps elongated to smooth, strong glides. At the end of the seven days, when Andy saw the routine, everything hit — the music, the movements, they even did flips on the ice. In fact, when the show was aired the Icecapades were interested enough to try to book the brothers for a few performances.

They learned a lot besides how to skate. They toured state fairs with Andy, and it was there that they learned to play instruments. "Jay," he was told, "I want you to play the drums on the next tour, and do a solo." The closest Jay had come to playing drums before this was hammering two spoons on a pan as a small child, but fortunately he had the talent. The family bought a drum set, and Wayne showed him how to play. In a week or two Jay played solo drums at a state fair. It was the hard way, but the pressure made learning a fast process.

Once a year the Osmonds managed a short vacation in their retreat, their refueling station — their farm in Huntsville, Utah. Here was "our haven away from the ersatz life of the west coast." When they were in the final miles of the journey to the old homestead they would strike up a song that Andy had made popular in his first years. Their paraphrase was "We're almost home, we're almost home, how wonderful, how wonderful that sound

With Andy Williams on TV

On tour in Japan in 1969

can be." A semblance of normality returned to life when they could feel the sod of home beneath their feet.

Here was fishing in the clean, clear streams of the upper Weber basin; stalking the elusive white-tail through the high, stinging air of the Uintah Mountains; following a flight of Canadian honkers into the marshes of Willard Bay. Here values could be reassessed and put into perspective. The smell of home-baked bread drifting out to the yard — a thousand images to be captured and filed away for those days when life would become a repetitive sameness. This for them was the recharging of the soul.

All too soon it was back to work. In California the family had been renting a home in Canoga Park, and this ran against the conservative grain of their makeup. They began to look for a house to buy. One day when Jay Williams and George Osmond were out together, Jay suddenly turned to George. "There's a house over on this next street that would be tremendous for your family. Nice big yard, large rooms. Tell you what, let's go in and talk to the ladies who own it, and if they'll sell. . . . Let's see! Tell you what we'll do. I'll flip you for the house. Either I'll buy it for Andy or you'll buy it for your family."

The car came to rest in front of a gingerbread, Spanish creation that reminded George of a Charles Addams cartoon. A tour of the premises did nothing to relieve his fear, a fear which was prompted by the knowledge that there's a 50 percent chance of losing when you flip a coin. He hoped the ladies would want to retain the property.

Have you ever gotten sick because you won something? George won the toss and felt a quiet panic seep over him. When he returned home that day he told the family to start packing. "We're going to move. I've bought a thirty-two-thousand-dollar monstrosity."

Olive agreed with his assessment, but the kids thought it was indeed a "neat" home. High ceilings, large doors, inlaid wooden floors, prismatic glass, banana trees. A widow's-walk type of railing around the roof. Curving wooden staircases. Archaic, slow, noisy plumbing. A bathtub which rested on claws. All in all it was a house that any child would love and most parents would abhor.

While the family lived in this home they paid a visit to Japan to make recordings and personal appearances. Jimmy, who was then of pre-school age, won the hearts of the Japanese people, whose graciousness showed through with a gift they made to him. The gift was an akita, and this dog had the distinction of being a grandson of the dog whose likeness appears on a national stamp of Japan. In honor of the volcanic crater near Tokyo, the boys called the dog Fujiyama.

Fuji had many interesting and occasionally questionable talents. He was an inveterate fence-jumper and he loved George's monstrosity for its multiplicity of nooks and crannies. He loved all the banana and bamboo trees and had a special feeling for the fire hydrant down the block. But most of all Fuji loved to jump fences.

One day the boys took him on the veranda and Fuji, spotting the railing around the edges, immediately accepted the challenge. Without any preparation he took off instantly for the hurdle. His "woof, woof, woof," signaled to all that he had lifted off and retracted his undercarriage. Up and over — but who had removed the ground? The initial "woof, woof, woof" soon progressed by several decibels, changing to "yipe, yipe, yipe," as the law of gravity asserted itself. Fuji was instantly cured of jumping fences, and thereafter whenever he longed for a stroll outside the confines of Arleta Drive he would wait patiently for someone to open the gate. If this assistance was

not forthcoming, he would content himself with the by no
means negligible mysteries of home.

Donny and Marie didn't go in for fence-jumping,
but they managed to find other distractions in this child's
dreamhouse. One of these was "dive bombing" the guest.
They secured pots and pans from the pantry, and when
people were coming into or going out of the house, these
miniature bombardiers unloaded their ammunition from
the upstairs porch. If they weren't quite on target, they
loosed another salvo from the inside balcony. The attacks
were discovered, however, and by special edict from the
war department Donny and Marie were drummed out of
military service; and their ammunition, which would
never again sit evenly on the stove, was confiscated and
assigned exclusively to the mundane role of cookery.

If you can't be a bombardier, you can at least be a
pirate. Now a pirate needs either something to dig up or
something to bury. Since Captain Donny Hook and First
Mate Marie Bluebeard didn't know of anything buried
around their "island," it stood to reason that they would
have to bury something. Mother's jewelry seemed the logical booty. It was appropriated from the upstairs bedroom,
neatly secured in a plastic breadwrapper, and buried at a
depth of two feet somewhere on that "desert isle." They
marked the burial spot with another plastic bag and went
in search of other plunder.

On that day gusts at the Los Angeles airport regis-
tered up to thirty miles per hour. Working its way out to
the Osmond neighborhood and weaving through the fence
on Arleta Drive, one of these gusts removed the marker.
Locating the burial spot and retrieving the booty was a
family project of considerable size. Captain Hook and Miss
Bluebeard were made to walk the plank of penance.

Fivesome look to the future

Future arrives for award-winning family —
(l. to r.) Merrill, Alan, Olive, George, Jay, Wayne,
Merrill's wife Mary, Donny, Jimmy, Marie

While Marie and Donny were vacillating between the "air force" and the "bounding main," Jay was strictly a cowboys and Indians man. If he didn't have anyone to play with at the time, it didn't bother him. He took both parts and would fall down clutching his chest where the fatal bullet had entered, then quickly rise and be acknowledged as the victor, placing his foot upon the imaginary body of the foe from whose position he had been so rapidly resurrected. Jay also liked to go over the railing on the second story, circle a banana tree with arms and legs, and be a fireman off to the rescue. One day he didn't wrap arms and legs to the tree as tightly as he should have, and like Fuji he found new respect for Newton's law. He eventually became more proficient, since another one of Donny and Marie's youthful distractions consisted of starting an occasional fire, and Jay more than once had to put these out.

Donny's recollections of those days is that they were "one long playtime," as they were also for Marie. The companionship of those who loved them. The inexhaustible resources of the refrigerator. Enough variety to pique the interest from sunup to sundown. An undiscovered nook to dream away the hours with those things which the young and imaginative need for flights of fancy. And finally a secure bed to regenerate cells, restore tired bodies, and rebuild tissues. This was enough for Donny and Marie at the time. They would have their own dates with destiny later.

For Donny especially, there wouldn't be long to wait for that date, for well before the expiry of the Osmonds' five-year contract with Andy Williams he would be anxious to "get into the act," and a year or so thereafter would be firmly installed. The boys worked with Andy periodically for about two years beyond the contract period, being billed as special guests in his TV shows. By

this time they had been clearly labeled as Andy's little
boys, and it would take a while to change that image. But
their national prominence was bringing them the book-
ings they needed in personal appearances around the nation.

By this time they were headliners — not yet in the
major cities, but in state fairs and in cities of 150,000
population or so. They were becoming known outside
America too; as well as tours in Japan, they toured Sweden
— in 1966, 1967, and 1968. They had a lot going for them.
They even split the billing with Phil Harris at fabled Las
Vegas. "Any time we had passed through Las Vegas over
the years, we would always say, 'Someday we'll see our
name up there in lights.' That was a big motivation to us."
Now this had been in a measure achieved. The Las Vegas
goal now was to headline there.

As a group nationally known and pushing for the
top, the logical step now was recordings. But that's a
different ballgame from personal appearances, and how
could they measure the potential audience? What kind of
following did they have?

While they were thinking this one through and
making some contacts in the recording industry, they received what looked like at least a partial answer to this
question. The brothers went on a promotion tour to Cleve-
land, Ohio, where in a Thanksgiving parade in freezing
temperatures they rode on a huge red fire engine. As the
parade proceeded it was clear that these boys were the
main attraction, as the squealing and jumping from the
girls on the sidelines showed. Why not get down there and
shake hands with the crowd! In a flash the boys were off
the fire truck and down among the people; and from then
on it was a pied piper situation, as the crowd closed in

behind the slow-moving fire engine and forgot the rest of the parade.

Later at Macys, where the boys were signing autographs, the crowd was so large that the police had to be called to disperse it. They got the kids out and closed the doors. Finally they had the brothers get on the roof and wave to the crowd below. This kind of popular acclaim would be repeated frequently in the future, with increasing elements of danger to both performers and fans, but this was the first time. "It was exciting," the boys recall. Now they began to realize that they had a following.

Around this time there was another development in the same direction. Working for a public relations firm the Osmonds had hired was a bright young teen-ager. He had a lot of good connections with teen magazines, and he began getting Osmond pictures in these periodicals. The readers caught on, started writing to the brothers. From this would later develop the Osmonds' own fan magazine.

The decision was made to go ahead on recordings, the first one being made in 1970. It didn't get off the ground. But "One Bad Apple" more than made up for it. The same week that that record hit the market, the Osmond CBS television special "He's My Brother" was aired. The boys didn't see that show — they were on their way to Japan. But Virl Osmond in the newly formed fan club was swamped with mail.

The summit was not far ahead. In 1971, true to their oft-expressed goal, they headlined at Caesar's Palace in Las Vegas. By 1974 they had twenty-two gold records lining their hallway. And the end was not yet.

3 Alan

A common advertising gimmick of a century or so ago featured an old and hackneyed phrase which still conjures up both childhood and antiquity. The picture showed a night-attired child kneeling in prayer at his bedside, his faithful mongrel beside him in reverential pose and with head cocked to one side. The caption read, "Now I lay me down to sleep."

At Fort Ord, California, this phrase came to Alan Osmond in a slightly corrupt form. Since early childhood he had always knelt in prayer before retiring. But this was his first day in the army and there were fifty recruits on his barracks floor. Might it not be politic to offer prayer silently from a horizontal position in bed?

A lifetime of habit made the decision for him and he knelt by his bunk and quietly offered his prayer. The loud noise hushed somewhat, but as he climbed into his bunk the buzzing started again.

> "Now I lay me down to sleep,
> A bag of peanuts at my feet.
> If I die before I wake,
> I know I'll die with the bellyache."

That barracks bard got the guffaws a wag of his eminence deserved.

The next day was occupied with checking out equipment, splitting up into formations, and generally getting organized. The wearisome day over, a tired band of recruits partook of the production-line cuisine and then filed into the barracks. After writing a brief but informative letter to his family, Alan picked up his towel and tooth-brush and went off to the vastness of the army's imper-sonal washroom. Upon his return he began to prepare for bed.

Since last night's prayers had gone rather well, he thought he'd go for two in a row. As he knelt, the buzzing increased. "He's gonna do it again," came a remark from the corner. "Wonder who he talks to!" "Say, as long as you're down there, say one for me." The noise grew as he prayed.

This went on for quite a while as Alan persisted nightly. But one evening as he knelt, suddenly from the bunk nearest the door came the command, "Shut up, you guys! Osmond's gonna say his prayers!" The long plain building became hushed. The toughest "hombre" in the company had issued an ultimatum. Alan completed his prayer and slid into bed. Because of his initial example, that "tough dude" would come to be Alan's friend, seek counsel and advice from him, and eventually follow his way of life.

As the oldest of the performing family, Alan is the spokesman, the director, the supervisor. He plays the role with warmth, consideration, charm, and firmness. In-itially he didn't seek the job, but he comes from a pa-triarchal order where it falls to the oldest to assume that responsibility. He keeps things going. In interview ses-sions of earlier days when the group were asked specific questions, they would all turn and look at Alan for the answer. As they have matured and grown to adulthood,

Alan Ralph Osmond

the others are perfectly capable of answering, and now no one really is the single spokesman for the group. Yet Alan's leadership while performing or rehearsing is still recognized. In addition he has branched out into the production end of the business and is gaining knowledge and experience there which will certainly come in handy somewhere down the line.

Alan has that natural flexibility to ad lib verbally or musically when someone has missed a cue. When that happens only the participants know that something has been added or deleted. This kind of stage presence takes years of experience to perfect. Yet there are times when nothing you do can correct a mistake. An example was that New Year's Eve in Florida.

Many famous and prominent people were in the audience, and as is customary in that type of gathering, Alan as the emcee was acknowledging the celebrities present. All went well until the last name. "And now, ladies and gentlemen, one of my favorite singers, a lady with a wall full of gold records," etc., etc. He went on and on. Alan did know this charming young lady and she was one of his favorites, as he had said, but when it came time to say her name, Connie Francis, he drew a blank on her last name and said — "here she is, Connie . . . . er . . . . ah . . . . Stevens." The audience knew he'd committed a faux pas because Connie Francis was standing. But coincidentally, to add to the confusion, on the far side of the room a lovely blonde girl rose to leave as the applause commenced. Alan's comment on that fiasco was, "When I saw two of them standing I could've swallowed my tongue." The next day he sent Connie Francis roses with a note of apology.

If you can't be sure of controlling your own tongue, Alan has discovered, you certainly don't know what someone else may do, even during a performance. The brothers have even had an occasional heckler introduce the competitive factor into their show by coming on or near the stage and singing with them, more often than not in a dissonant key. Interestingly enough, such an impromptu performer usually thinks he is pretty good.

According to Alan, that's not the only kind of competition performers experience. "In Las Vegas there are people who come right up on the front row and take pictures. If they can get outside with the film, they take the negatives and make posters to sell. I've watched the bouncers take the cameras away from them, take the film out, and give them the cameras back.

"In this business there are those who like to leech off your efforts. In Europe there seems to be no way of stopping the poster companies from capitalizing on your pictures. They will sneak in and take pictures of you, then blow them up on giant posters and sell them. There just aren't laws tight enough to protect you from this, so there are these type of people all over. We've walked out of concerts and run into "I love Donny" signs, T shirts with our pictures on them, and things like that, things that never came through our organization."

If people do that with the "fringe" material, what do they do with the central product, the Osmonds' musical productions? "They bootleg our albums all the time. In this respect we are one of the hardest-hit acts in the business. They buy a record, take it to their little underground-type studio, make their own tapes, put a picture of us on them, and sell them. In the United States of course the copyright laws are supposed to protect performers from this infringement, but it would be very difficult to locate all the offenders, and by the time we had taken them all to court we'd spend more money than we'd ever make by selling records. It's kind of a bad part of the business.

"This bootlegging of records and tapes is very bad, especially down South. We put out a souvenir-type album where we pressed only about a thousand at the most and another one of five hundred copies which contained our hit records. These were for disc jockeys and the press people. We signed and numbered each one and kept a list of those we gave them to. The next thing we knew, copies of them were on sale in some store. The picture had been copied from the album and was poorer in quality, and I'm sure the quality of the record was down as well. That's the thing that upsets us most, because in paying for a poor-quality reproduction the consumer gets hurt."

Alan admits that the enjoyable, even humorous happenings outweigh those negative ones. "We enjoy giving autographs as long as the crowd is reasonable, though when they begin to snatch at everything and you see the reasoning leave their eyes, it's time to make a hasty exit." Girls have been known to be less than calm when asking for an autograph, the excitement causing them to stammer or even to twist words around. "Oh, you are my greatest fan!" one may say, or "Will you give me my autograph?" The Osmonds know that fans are important to a musical group, but they don't look on them merely as commercial assets. To them their fans are warm human beings; and although they can be rather dangerous en masse, the individual fan who chances to meet Alan or any other Osmond is sure of a courteous and friendly response.

When he was younger, Alan tended to be shy and somewhat reticent about pushing himself forward, and in these circumstances his journal became special in his life. Here he could retreat to his "someone to talk to," pour out his feelings to his "favorite friend." He began to write

It's business at the phone

It's relaxation in the family speedboat

simple verse when he was ten, a beginning which helped him in later years to become a proficient songwriter. Even when quite young he was interested in music, and he would follow his father about, hoping to hear him break into song so that Alan might join in. In those years too he developed his ear to where he could hear the harmony and could sing an alto part.

In the sixth grade Alan learned to read music, and before reaching high school age he had mastered the rudiments of string bass, trumpet, ukelele, and guitar. It's fortunate that in the sixth grade his musical talent was noticed, because while in the fifth grade he had been set for a career as a scientist. He had a rather large rock collection in one corner of the house, where he set up his chemistry set and microscope and prepared to be the first man on the moon.

In junior high school he enjoyed Latin, French and Spanish, mathematics and art. Something he didn't particularly enjoy was that he changed junior high schools six times. "Friends aren't that easy to come by."

Much of the brothers' education has been obtained from tutors, for the law required that they have a tutor when not attending regular school. The boys were not slow to notice tutorial idiosyncrasies. "When we were on tour, we had to take the tutor with us wherever we went, and there was one tutor whose main claim to fame was that as our tutor he had the power to stop the show. He would tell the newspaper reporters that. Other than that he wasn't too much trouble. He used to fall asleep quite a bit, and then I'd have to take over school." Alan chuckles. "We sure had a lot of parties!"

The schedule required by the family's chosen career was bound to exact its toll on "normal" living. Alan didn't see a basketball game until he was out of high school. He didn't see a baseball game until the family went to Japan on a tour. But he did spend countless hours practicing songs, learning routines — then, when he had the parts down, his voice would change and he would have to learn new parts. Of course it was all grist to the mill, for the many hours he spent revoicing harmonies helped him to gain a good knowledge of and feel for music in a relatively short time.

Always interested and increasingly capable in the field of electricity, Alan spent much time helping Donny to develop that skill. He admits that Donny has exceeded his expectations. "We've had professional electronic help that didn't know as much as Donny. He's become the family's personal electrician." Alan built a darkroom and soon began to develop color slides. "I love photography and hope some day to publish a book with pictures and some of my poetry."

Although his father and mother had sold everything to advance the boys' singing careers, they knew that Alan had always wanted to go on a mission for his Church. They backed his desire 100 percent — no small matter, since this would mean completely financing him for two years as well as losing him from the group for that period. But as the time of decision drew near, his local draft board wanted him to go on a mission for them. Alan Osmond is a patriot; he supports his country. He also supports his Church. What was he to do? He made the decision a matter of prayer and received his answer. One day the phone rang. It was a friend of his. He had been thinking of Alan, he said, and wondered where Alan stood in the draft. Alan explained the situation. "Isn't that strange?" the friend said. He explained that he had a friend in the National Guard who had told him earlier that day that there was one opening in the Guard in the whole of Southern California.

The next day Alan was to report to his draft board, but now he checked in at the local armory first. The commanding officer was about to leave his office for the day but he decided to talk to Alan. He liked what he saw and signed Alan up. By this unusual turn of events Alan missed by a matter of hours a two-year stint in the regular army and the high probability of service in Vietnam. He became instead a "weekend soldier" for six years, with two weeks out of each year to be spent in camp. Six months of basic training would come first.

This was the only time Alan has been away from his family for any extended period. "On the whole I rather enjoyed it," he says. In the army he was confronted with just about every tinge in the human spectrum, including those whose level of decency was precisely in inverse proportion to the prevailing temptations. He began to earn their respect that first night when he knelt to pray in a roomful of non-kneelers. The process wasn't harmed any by his qualifying with the top score on the rifle range. "I've always competed in a sense, and here I was in the service. I felt that urge for competition and I determined to do my best."

An advantage of being absent from the other four brothers was that now Alan could be accepted for himself, so he didn't at first reveal his identity. When someone would ask, "Hey, are you related to those brothers that sing?" he would just smile and beat around the bush in his answer. But it finally got out. The brothers were doing a series of Jerry Lewis shows and Alan went over to the company orderly room to watch one of them on TV. He was proud of what he saw, and this time when someone asked if he was related to those guys singing on the screen, he said, "Yeah, those are my brothers."

Now the cat was loose. The next morning on parade it was "Osmond, front and center" from the first sergeant. He ran to the sergeant and stood at attention.

"Sing us a song, kid."

Another decision to be made. It came after only a slight pause, "No, sir! I'm a soldier."

Alan remembers the shade of red which crept up toward the sergeant's ears. The voice boomed again, "Osmond, sing us a song."As firmly as the previous refusal, "No, sir! I'm a soldier."

That afternoon and evening Alan became acquainted with various assortments of culinary apparatus. He washed big pans, little pans, in-between pans, tools he'd never seen before and found hard to believe could be used in the kitchen. He took his wrinkled hands to bed long after the lights were out in his barracks.

On early parade the next morning, in that misty dawn off the coast of California, he again heard his name . "Osmond, front and center."

Double time up to the first sergeant, snap to attention.

"Osmond, sing us a song."

There was no delay this time, "No, sir! I'm a soldier."

That day he was reintroduced to the duties of a scullerymaid. That day he rose inestimably in the esteem of his fellow soldiers.

That wasn't the last temptation to be a singing soldier. A young officer struck up an acquaintance with Alan and used his influence to get him exempted from physical training. Actually Alan enjoyed P.T., but he went along with this on the assumption that there was something else he was required to do. (There was — but not the kind of thing he thought.) This man also got him excused from the tedious and boring job of clean-up, a job where you are required to pick up everything that isn't moving and to salute everything that is.

When the officer took Alan home to dinner and introduced him to his wife and children, even to new-soldier Osmond this seemed a bit irregular. He soon found out the reason for these attentions. The officer was a fledgling songwriter, and Alan's skills and status in the entertainment world were just right for performing the officer's songs — with both of them singing, of course — at a big bash for the officers.

Alan had no trouble in finding the answer. "Sir, I can't do it. I'm under contract. And there are a few other principles I'd be violating." Clean-up detail and P.T. were first on his agenda the next day.

At the end of his basic training, besides ranking number one with the rifle, he had received the highest score among the trainees in a test of his overall knowledge. A rather uncommon young man who was voted by officers and non-commissioned officers alike as the outstanding trainee of the camp.

Uncommon young men are apt to be attracted to uncommon young women, even if it takes a few years to find the right one. Alan found his girl in Suzanne Pinegar.

He went out with many before that, some of them very fine girls, he recalls. One of them, a cheerleader, got him a second-row ticket for a basketball game at Brigham Young University, but it was another cheerleader, blonde, blue-eyed and beautiful, who made the most points. Dur-

With
Suzanne —
always

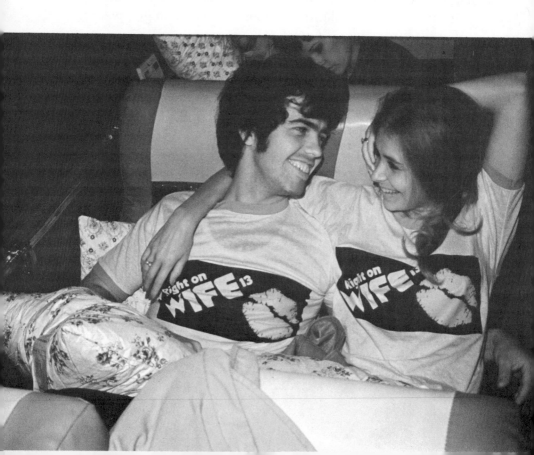

ing the game Alan's eyes kept wandering to her, and somehow hers kept moving to him. When the glances met, each quickly looked away. This kind of game is much older than basketball — and much more fun.

After the game Alan moved down to the front, talked to one or two others, hung around till Suzanne was available. He introduced himself. The lady played it cool. "I thought, well, this is kind of exciting, but he gets attention from girls all the time. I just acted as if he was any other guy."

There came dates together and dates each had with others. There was much talk, exploration of mutual thinking, attitude, conviction. In the next few months the "tender trap" gradually closed on both of them — a little quicker on Alan than on Suzanne.

The signs were good, but was this enough? The matter was too important for casual decision. It required higher counsel. In prayer Alan sought guidance from the Power which had never failed him. The answer was strong and clear.

"We had been swimming with Jay and others," Suzanne recalls, "and I had accidentally scraped my chin on the bottom. When we got dressed, there I was in levis, straggly hair, with no makeup and a scraped-up chin — and it was then that Alan proposed to me."

It was a bit quick for Suzanne, and she had to have a little time for the answer. She too had to have her assurance from the same Power Alan had consulted. A few days later he picked her up, and as they drove along she said, "Alan, I've made a decision."

He looked over to her.

"Yes," said Suzanne.

The car screeched to a halt in the middle of the road. "Yahoo," yelled Alan. Then he reached out and embraced her.

They were married in the Mormon Temple at Provo. The ceremony sealed them to each other as man and wife forever — not just till death parts them, but beyond that and into the eternities ahead.

Now that he had found her, Alan Osmond wouldn't have it any other way.

It was a beautiful, clear day in fall, and Mother Nature's paintbrush was ablaze with golds and yellows, browns and reds. A quiet peaceful day in the austere grandeur of the Tetons, it was a day when man was painting his own hideous images and blood-red colors across western Europe, where World War I was in its fourth year. On that thirteenth day of October 1917, the progenitor of a very unusual family came into the world and exercised his talents for the first time. In that initial plaintive, short, high-rpm rattle of the newborn, George Virl Osmond, Sr., inflated his diaphonous lungs and, with the clean air of Star Valley as a catalyst, began to practice those notes which in years to come would be systematically taught to his children.

Etna, Wyoming, is located in the west central portion of Wyoming in cattle and farm country. Harsh, cold winters and warm, gentle summers have etched their scroll across the landscape. George spent his early years in Wyoming and San Diego until in his youth he received greetings from President Roosevelt and an invitation to assist in again making the world safe for democracy. When he was released from active duty in January 1944, because of a persistent stomach problem, World War II was still raging. George turned up at a military depot in Ogden, Utah, looking for employment.

"He was wearing his uniform, and I thought I had never seen anyone quite so handsome." These were the thoughts of Olive Davis as she first saw George Osmond talking to a friend and co-worker. He was introduced to Olive as "a former high school student of mine from Star Valley, Wyoming." After that brief encounter, Olive Davis wrote in her diary that night, "Today I met someone who's going to mean a lot to me." A prophetic understatement indeed! George Osmond could not know it, but the die had been cast and he had met "that girl" — the one who would assist him in creating "the tightest blend of brother harmony in show business."

As girls tend to be in matters of the heart, Olive was a good deal quicker in sensing the direction life was to take. She looks back with these words: "One late afternoon, a few days after our first meeting, I was in the post restaurant doing some bookkeeping for them, when I heard, 'Hi, Jo, are you working hard?' (He has called me Jo through the years.) I instantly knew that voice, although I'd only heard it once before. As I turned to meet him, I seemed to nearly melt. I suddenly felt as though I'd known him a lifetime. I suppose I fell in love with him right there."

When Olive talked to her mother about George, it turned out that her mother not only knew the Osmonds of Star Valley but had actually lived in their home for a while — had even carried George around as a toddler. She had several photos of the family. This coincidence was almost unbelievable to both George and Olive. What would it do to their relationship? When she showed George photos bearing his mother's handwriting and told him the story, Olive felt that he gave her some quizzical looks, as if afraid there was something going on that he was not sure about. But he kept turning up in the restaurant. "I noticed he kept

glancing my way when eating," says Olive, "and sometimes I found him sitting back in his chair and studying
me. I wondered if he felt as I did — that perhaps our
meeting was somehow arranged by Providence long before we ever met."

George was now busy at two jobs, sometimes working around the clock, so he had little time for dating. Olive
would occasionally catch a hello or a goodbye as he was
going to or coming from a job. But one day he stopped by
her home while she was playing the piano. The incident is
etched on her memory: "He walked over and put his hand
lightly on my shoulder, and I can still remember the thrill
that went through me. Then he began to sing. If you could
have heard his voice on that day you'd know just where the
boys get their singing talent. It was clear, mellow, beautiful. I played on and he sang on. It was a wonderful afternoon." She adds, "I wondered if he was ever going to ask
me for a date."

As friendship developed, George confided that at
twenty-six and with poor health he had decided he must
remain a bachelor so as not to be a burden on anyone. This
aroused Olive's maternal instinct. Her family doctor was
also George's doctor. It was no trick at all to find out from
him secretly that all George needed was "some good home
cooking and tender loving care." Olive "was careful not to
tell George about this incident until after the wedding.
Boys don't like girls who snoop."

Finally that first date came: an Abbott and Costello
movie, then to Ogden's White City ballroom where one of
the "big bands" was playing — no less than Tommy Dor-
sey. This was voted a great evening. Both musically
oriented, they enjoyed dancing — especially with each
other.

It's not too surprising that around this time George's half-formed resolve not to marry began to weaken. Olive's subtle campaign to change his mind was nudging him in the right direction when he suffered an accident — in falling from a moving train while at work as a brakeman. While recovering from a severely sprained ankle, he went to California to "think things over." About a week later, Olive received a letter which contained the line: "I'm glad I found you. If you think you love me enough, let's make some serious plans."

Olive's elation at this robbed her of discretion, and she told friends of the glad news. As it rapidly spread, she regretted her folly. How would George react when he found she had shared his letter — and he not even totally sold on marriage?

When George returned and heard the talk going around, he was quiet, subdued, somewhat distant with Olive. Was he reverting, or was he still thinking things over? There were no dates, no confidential chats. Olive wondered whether she should try to forget the whole thing and seek dates with others, but her heart said this was impossible.

One day her friend Belva asked for help. Dear friends of hers were to visit Ogden, she said. Would Olive please be the date for one of them at dinner? With mixed emotions, Olive agreed — perhaps it would shake George up, bring the situation to a head one way or the other.

At the appointed hour, outwardly glowing in a new dress and hairdo, Olive awaited her blind date in her living room. At a knock she opened the door and there stood George. "Hi, Jo. I hear you're stepping out on me tonight, and I don't know if I like it or not."

"Well, I didn't know you cared," Olive retorted

rather sarcastically. "You certainly haven't bothered to tell me."

"Oh, it's all right," he said. "This guy's Belva's friend, and I know you're just going as a favor to her. I came over to pick you up, since everyone is meeting over at Belva's."

Just like that. Not even jealous, thought Olive. She grabbed her wrap and walked stiffly to the car.

The rest of this story is best told in Olive's words. "No one was in evidence when we entered Belva's living room, but a card table which bore candles and flowers was set for two. Suddenly a warm happy feeling came over me. This was no blind date. Belva and George had arranged it; and she had cooked dinner and left for the evening. My heart jumped up to my throat. I fairly tingled.

"We ate dinner by candlelight and danced to the radio. I felt quite special. As we were dancing, George said, 'I've brought you a little something, but you'll have to find it.' After he had gently steered me in that direction it took me about three seconds to find a small, neatly wrapped package behind a picture on the mantel. I opened it with trembling hands — and stared open-mouthed at a diamond engagement ring. Now I wondered if my heart would leap out of my throat. I laughed and cried at the same time. In one split second my prayers and dreams had all come true. . . ."

Not long after this the couple were married in the Salt Lake Temple. George now left the railroad and, being a good carpenter, got a job in construction work. But to him pounding nails was dead-end, monotonous work and his drive and ambition couldn't take it for long as a full-time job, so he quit. Around the same time Olive quit her job too, as pregnancy made her too ill and miserable to continue. George got a job servicing accounts for a radio station. With the money they had diligently saved they bought a two-acre lot and began plans for building a house.

On October 19, 1945, George and Olive became parents. They named the baby George Virl Osmond, Jr. From the start Olive took motherhood very seriously — with her first child she was, she says, a "very nervous mother." With the bassinet right by her side of the bed she would wake and listen for Virl's breathing. The light rattle she heard one day in his chest could have been a cold picked up in the hospital, but was it? A friendly neighbor cautioned the parents — the baby's hard breathing could be a serious condition caused by an enlarged thymus gland, a gland which has some control of a child's growth and development before birth but is supposed to shrink after birth, and sometimes does so only slowly or even continues to grow. The neighbor had lost a baby through this. Sure enough, an x-ray revealed that Virl had this problem. The doctor prescribed x-ray treatments which seemed to clear it up.

If Olive was at first a nervous mother, George (like most new fathers who have not been around babies) was almost scared stiff to touch the baby for fear of hurting him. But particularly when they had passed the tiny, delicate stage, he has enjoyed all his children immensely. After that stage too he was certainly not afraid to touch them when he felt they needed disciplining. Olive, whose parents had never raised a hand to her, had a hard job getting used to this. She recalls: "He used to say, as he would tan their britches, 'Mother, the Lord gave us these children to raise properly, to teach them and train them. How are you going to do that if you spoil them rotten and let them have their own way?' Sometimes the discussion on this point

The wedding day

Virl — the first of the nine

got rather heated, and he would add a few choice words about having to raise me too, then I would go off and sulk."

How did this come out? Again, we had better let Olive explain: "I had always recognized that the husband is the head of the household, and since I respected that authority I would always give in. But later I would give a double dose of sympathy to the child concerned. Consequently for over thirty years I have been spoiling them and he has been straightening them out."

George acknowledges that to some extent he had to push the boys in the early years, and he is loud in his praise for Olive's gentle counteractive influence. There has never been any argument about the two parents' respective roles. To the family, the father's position is axiomatic, and they express it in these words: "Father may not always be right, but he is always Father." Time has vindicated the merits of his training, which he adhered to regardless of what weaker mortals might counsel. Olive recalls: "In show business, when we were working on the TV sets and so on, people would often advise us to have the boys 'loosen up,' not to say 'Yes, sir,' and 'Yes, ma'am.' But George would say, 'They're going to be respectful, they're going to say "Yes, sir," and "Yes, ma'am." ' They're polite today because of that kind of training." To Olive, the secret of family unity is to have a good, strong father at the head. To the observer, another secret of this family's success is the progressive spirit of both parents. They are never bored or boring but always involved in something worthwhile.

Although George has been a strict father, the children have always known that the strictness sprang from his love for them and the great responsibility he felt to train them properly. Olive and the nine children freely acknowledge that he has never hesitated to tell them or show them his love in many different ways. He has never been too busy to take time out to play with them — everything from playing cowboy down on his knees as a horse, to wrestling sometimes three or four at a time, or to having a game of baseball. He has had them by his side whenever he was busy doing things, so that they could learn from his knowledge and skills — wiring a house, changing a tire, doctoring an animal, driving a tractor, repairing the plumbing, putting a worm on a hook. In fact, no small part of the skills the Osmond brothers have today are a result of the "on-the-job" training their father has given them in earlier years.

"A wise Providence gave us eight boys and one girl, in that proportion," says Olive. "I don't think I would have been as knowledgeable in training that many girls as George has been with the boys. I have a tendency to spoil, to wait on them, and not make them pick up and do for themselves. George used to call me the Little Red Hen. But in time I learned."

The year 1946 was a successful one, as George's sales of radio advertising swelled the family bank account and financed a new car — a black Dodge which was George's pride and joy. In August, Olive entered Virl in a local baby contest and he won. In her excitement she narrowly missed wrecking the new car on the way home.

Having proved his salesmanship abilities, by the spring of 1947 George decided to get into real estate. South of Ogden, in Riverdale, they found a house with an acre of ground and moved in. George enjoyed his new occupation and did well in it. As with his previous job, Olive again became his secretary.

But 1947 had its problems too. Pregnant for the second time, Olive came down with the measles — a worrying thing for an expectant mother. Virl caught them

The
baby-contest
winner

George holds Tom while Virl watches for the "birdie"

too. That summer Olive's parents were in a nasty road accident which nearly took their lives, and after a long time in the hospital they came to George and Olive's to recuperate. And to top it off, the doctor told Olive that she had RH negative blood and that there could therefore be complications in childbirth.

It turned out that there were no complications on that account when, as his mother describes him, "a beautiful chubby-cheeked, brown-eyed little boy joined us on October 26, 1947." The new baby fitted in well. Virl and Tom were pals right from the start and have been extremely close through the years.

About this time opportunity knocked again in the shape of an offer to George of a real estate and insurance agency of his own in Cedar City, in Southern Utah. Tom was two weeks old when they made the decision to go. Not long after they arrived the parents noticed in Tom's chest the rattling noise that Virl had had. They drove the three hundred miles back to Ogden to the doctor who had treated Virl, and Tom received the same diagnosis — enlarged thymus gland — and the same x-ray treatments. But during treatment the baby's hand knocked the machine and it then directed the rays to his neck and ear. No one knew how long it had been in that position. Olive in particular recalls the gnawing fear she had that something terrible had happened.

The Cedar City office at first had seemed to have plenty of secretarial help, but when George got busy selling, Olive's services were again required in his business. Working in their apartment, she typed insurance policies, answered correspondence, and generally took care of office matters. How about housekeeping? George knew that that must be a secondary concern in these circumstances. "I wanted Olive right by my side," he said, "and so long as she took care of the children properly, that was the main thing. In my experience I had already discovered that women as a rule know very little about business matters. I wanted Olive to learn all she could about such things, so that if anything happened to me she would be able to take care of herself and the boys."

It soon became apparent that the man who had offered George an option on the agency, seeing the booming sales, had prudently decided to "let George do it" — to retain his interest as a partner rather than sell out. This didn't sit at all well with George and Olive. They were out to build their own business, not someone else's. Promptly they decided to move back to Ogden and set up for themselves. When someone offered them a twenty-seven-foot trailer house, the next day they bought it; and soon they were Ogden-bound again.

In the city they called home they bought a piece of property in the north end of town and got construction going on a small office building for their own real estate and insurance office. Their first account was a florist. "To this day," says George, "any time we drive past our old building, one of us is bound to say, 'That's where we started our business.' "

Ambitious and hard-working, George threw himself into the task of making the business a success. His friendly way brought him good sales both in real estate and insurance, and the business slowly grew. Learning more about the business all the time, Olive here learned something also about life. While she kept the books for their business, as an extra source of income she did some typing for an elderly man who was selling oil stock. Several months after she had begun working for him she still hadn't been paid. Finally she had to ask for payment. She recalls: "He convinced me I should take oil stock instead.

It would only be a short time till the well came in. 'A gusher,' he assured me. I took the stock, and the well did turn out to be a gusher — a gusher of salt water! It was my first lesson that gambling doesn't pay."

By fall that year George and Olive were a little tired of trailer living, so when someone came into the office and wanted to trade his equity in a brick home for a trailer, they struck a deal. The house was dirty and run down and took a lot of scrubbing, remodeling, painting and floor covering before it was the way they wanted it. But it had a fenced yard at the back for the children. "I think that's what sold us on the place," Olive recalls. "George built them a nice sandbox and we bought a little tricycle. I can still see Virl peddling that tricycle and Tommy standing on the back, his arms around Virl's waist, head thrust back to enjoy the passing scenery. They would circle the yard by the hour without either of them tiring."

It was in this home that a sad discovery was made. The sandbox was just outside the window, so when Olive was working in the house she could listen for the sounds of the boys and occasionally go out and check on them. She noticed that when she called them, only Virl would look up and answer. Tommy wouldn't pay any attention. Yet when she crossed his vision, he would look up and smile at her. She knew he was a quiet boy, but she wondered, for the first time, if perhaps he couldn't hear. The thought frightened her.

In Ogden there is a very fine school for the deaf, and she now took Tommy there for a hearing test. Since Virl had been somewhat slow in learning to talk, mispronounced his "r's," and was not saying some of his words right, she decided to take him along too. She felt sure there was nothing wrong with Virl but had a strong urge to have him tested also.

Olive looks back on the experience in these words: "I remember how calm the young man was who talked to me about the test. He was businesslike without being cold. As he laid it out for me in specifics, I thought how like a movie this was. Surely I must be observing it all from a distance; and it had nothing to do with me or my family. I felt as though I was projected upon a scene where the melodrama was gripping the audience and I had somehow become a part of it. I refused to believe what he was saying. His voice came from a hollow chamber. An icy fist knotted in my stomach. Helplessness consumed me.

" 'Are you sure? They're both shy boys, and perhaps you've made a mistake?'

"The realization of what he was saying finally seeped through. Virl with his crooked grin and extraordinary patience had only 50 percent of his hearing; and Tommy, with his large brown eyes and quiet gentleness, was hard deaf.

"I choked back the tears and felt the salty residue in my throat. My life had changed in such a way that the days now past could never be totally recalled without some pain. I began to prepare myself and my two children for a life where soft, gentle sounds and the subtle nuances of the aural world would drift past them unheard."

5   Wayne

To Kathlyn White that day began just like an ordinary Sunday — that is, if any day could be "ordinary" to a girl whose beauty and talents had won her the titles of Miss Dairy Princess, Miss Davis County, Miss Utah State Fair and Miss Utah, to say nothing of the excitement of the Miss America pageant in Atlantic City. Here she was back in Provo, Utah, a student at Brigham Young University on a one-year scholarship she had inexplicably accepted in preference to a four-year scholarship at another university. As she walked to church with friends that morning, all the beauty of late spring was in the air and the world looked good.

Later that day she was back in church for the evening service, where she was to sing a solo. An accomplished singer, she moved many a soul in the congregation that evening with her melodious rendition. To one listener, a dark-haired, brown-eyed young man of twenty-two, the effect was electric. "I *have* to meet her," he said to himself. He had come with another girl, and normally would have expected to give that girl his total attention. But the urge was irresistible, and when the service was over he excused himself for a moment and made his way to Kathy.

Melvin Wayne Osmond

"I'm Wayne Osmond," he told her. "I just had to tell you how much I enjoyed your solo. You have a beautiful voice."

Etiquette forbade too lengthy a conversation then, since the other girl was waiting for him, but before leaving Kathy he had managed to elicit her address and phone number. A week later he phoned her. Would she like to go flying with him? Indeed she would. Schedules were difficult to mesh at that point, but a week after that Kathy was introduced to Wayne's Cessna 182 and to some of his skills as a pilot.

"She lived in apartment 21," Wayne recalls, "and I'd go and see her all the time and prevent her from doing her school work. We dated a lot — on and off at first, but more consistently as time went on. I even let her go home for the summer, and what with that and the group being on tour I only saw her for one day in that three months."

They made up for lost time when Kathy returned to Provo in the fall, and shortly Wayne proposed. A December wedding was in his mind, but for Kathy it perhaps wasn't quite that easy. "Why can't we wait?" was her first thought. She took only twenty-four hours to determine that marrying rather than waiting was the right course.

Why the initial thought to the contrary? "Well, I was Miss Utah, after all, and I would have to resign from that position if I got married. Naturally there is a certain prestige in being Miss Utah, and I'd been very thrilled to receive that honor among forty-seven contestants. I'd worked for this for a long time — music lessons, modeling classes, and so on — ever since a Miss Utah came to my class when I was in the eighth grade. I'd been to the Miss America pageant and had a lot of fine opportunities, all good learning experiences, and I knew there would be

Bride and bridegroom (Salt Lake Temple in background)

With his
other love –
the Cessna 182

At the wedding reception . . .

. . . and in later days

others down the road. You just don't lightly give up something like that.''

So why give it up? ''I suppose I just put a higher priority on marriage. That's forever, whereas the excitement of being a beauty queen lasts only for a few months.''

This former beauty queen has some interesting reflections on the subject of beauty in women. ''Sometimes I'm disappointed at the emphasis people put on physical beauty. First of all, girls who have it are often liked for their outward appearance alone, which is a pretty shallow approach. Not that it's not important for a girl to be well groomed, to make the most of herself, because it *is*. But boys should look deeper than that. I know I've had roommates who didn't get dates because of this emphasis, while actually they were a lot more beautiful overall than some girls who were admired for their physical appearance.''

Clearly Wayne is a lucky fellow. With Kathy, there's both inward and outward beauty. And he got his December wedding too — December 1974, in the Salt Lake Temple.

Kathy had dated several other fellows before Wayne, but she rates the first date with him as certainly the most unusual of them all. After all, on how many first dates do the couple go joy-riding in the young man's plane? The story behind this foremost of Wayne's offstage interests (apart from Kathy and his family) has some unusual facets.

''Mother would drive me to the airport and I'd hop into my Cessna 182 and fly for four or five hundred miles. What a place for contemplation! There was a great poem written by an air force officer during World War II. I remember portions of it.

> 'Oh, I have slipped the surly bonds of earth,
> Put out my hand and touched the face of God.'

There is that feeling of exultation that comes with flying which I have never felt anywhere else.

"After I'd log five hundred miles or so I'd land back at the airport and call Mother to come and get me. I know it's a bit backwards, but I had my pilot's license almost two years before I had my driver's license. I just didn't care for driving. As a matter of fact, my twentieth birthday was upon me before I took the driver's test. If it weren't a necessity I wouldn't have troubled to get a driver's license."

For that first date Kathy had some previous information which didn't seem to hold up. "I had met Alan and Jay about four months previously, and I'd asked them if they didn't have another brother. 'Yes, we have,' they told me, 'but he likes to stay at home and clean guns.' Later I was told Wayne was shy and reserved, but he wasn't that way with me, and he didn't seem at all anxious to get back to his guns. I remember how warm and friendly he was and how he didn't seem to be at all reticent about talking."

This is unusual, because Wayne is known as a good listener and will politely hear someone out. For all that, he is his own man. He will not agree with something just to be courteous. He has mature and sound judgment and takes a strong stand for what he thinks is right.

No one can remember having a serious argument with Wayne. He is a strong stabilizing force in the group and has been known to calm down the more expressive. He places no barriers on friendship and gets along well with everyone. So far as he knows, he has no enemies. "I have no need for enemies," he says. He has found, within himself, the ability to like everyone.

This gentle personality obviously does not spring from a placid, do-nothing life. From earliest years Wayne has always been intensely involved in life. On stage and in recordings he is the professional singer, sax player and guitarist. Off stage he does his share of songwriting — together with Alan and Merrill, for example, he composed the lyrics and music for the group's 1974 album "The Plan," which they describe as a "statement of belief." He likes to build gadgets and repair what needs repairing. And he's an avid and capable mechanic.

As with his brothers, it was personal drive that developed such skills. With his flying hobby in mind, when Wayne realized that his tutors were not going far enough beyond the "reading, 'riting and 'rithmetic" stage of his education, he taught himself geometry, trigonometry and calculus. It required a great deal of self-motivation to master the higher mathematics in this way, but he wanted to be a flight instructor, and to do this he had to pass his private aircraft, commercial aircraft and instrument-flying tests. These are now behind him, and when the family is at home base in Utah he has twenty students to whom he teaches the rudiments of flying.

"We need to set goals for ourselves," he says. "It isn't hard if you have a goal. I must be motivated or I can't accomplish anything. So often a person finds out, too late, that he should have been striving to reach a plateau, then another, and another. If we just stand still we can't be content." Such principles have been stressed by theologians, economists, educators and salesmen throughout the ages. Wayne is one of the relatively few who practice them.

How did he get hung up on flying? When he was three his father took him to an air show to watch the famed Blue Angels, the navy's precision flying team. He knew then that what he saw were airplanes and that what he wanted to do was fly. By his thirteenth birthday Andy

Working with the group

With Jimmy,
doing leather work

With ice cream, doing no work

Williams had given him his first flying lesson, and the next year he took the controls of a plane with an instructor beside him. "It was a Cherokee 140, and I still recall that thrill as the instructor allowed me to lay my hands and feet on the controls. Knowing that the thrust against the air was supporting the craft and I was giving it direction was somehow almost a spiritual feeling to me."

Around his eighteenth birthday he received his private pilot license, and shortly afterwards he had to quit flying for a while because of a step-up in the group's engagements. Since qualifying as a private pilot, he has advanced through multi-engine rating. He takes his instructor responsibilities seriously. "If I have a student who is not understanding what I'm trying to convey, I look to myself first. Perhaps it's my fault. I rephrase or reexplain whatever I was trying to teach." Wayne recognizes that there are different levels of comprehension and treats his students as individuals.

He has had only one close call as a pilot or instructor, and he strongly feels that 99 percent of air accidents are pilot-caused. The pilot must be on his toes to maintain control. "There are things called stalls where the airplane loses maneuverability because of lack of speed. There are several kinds of stalls, each having a different effect and requiring different corrective action. You just about have to let your students learn by their mistakes. Every once in a while they will put you in a tailspin and you start yelling, as if you're frightened, 'Oh! what did you do?' Actually a tailspin is easily handled, but it is just a little frightening the first time you are in one. As instructor I'll kind of sit back and let it happen, because I like to see the reaction of my student. A tailspin also can be a great teacher, especially to a cocky student. Cockiness is a bad attitude for a pilot to have, so without doing anything mean or abrupt

I'll sometimes help a cocky student into a tailspin by my own actions and let him try to get it out. I'm pleased at the new-found respect the student has for the airplane. That is usually the end of goofing around."

To further his flying skills, Wayne has taken lessons in aerobatic airplanes, and this has confirmed his strong feeling that if you respect your craft it will respond in like manner. "The greatest number of fatalities in private planes, according to the Civil Aeronautics Board, is caused by the pilots getting lost. That means pilot error — like flying in poor weather conditions, or not keeping up with flying after they've got their license."

How about the engine quitting? "Engines do quit through human error. Of all things, some people actually run out of gas. Or they allow moisture to get in the fuel line and condense. These and other poor pilot techniques will cause the engine to cease and desist. But simple mechanical failure of a well-maintained engine — almost never."

Wayne knows something of the dangers of pilot error, for his one close call came from that source. He was turning down-wing on a base leg final approach when something told him to look down. He did, and saw his left wheel just about touching the roof of another airplane. He had been cleared for the landing, but some unthinking pilot had sneaked in underneath him, presumably because he didn't want the bother of going through the control tower. A sharp pull on the stick got Wayne out of danger.

Wayne's rather expensive hobby has been made possible by the gains from show business, a chosen career which he enjoys to the full. But the trappings of fame and fortune have made no impression on him. He has a strong spiritual leaning and is more impressed with where he's going than where he's been. "There's a song with a line in it that goes, 'I have wandered from a more exalted sphere.' Material things of this life have never really troubled me much because I really feel that the greatest goal is to get back home, back to where we came from.''

He realizes that young people do not want to be preached at. "No one wants to be told how to live his life. But a lot of young people act very negatively about life, and I believe that frequently this is their way of saying, 'Here I am, brother, help me.' I believe that ultimately that help can only come from God, and certainly he is the source of my own positive way of living.''

Despite his strong convictions, Wayne has taught himself through the years never to argue religion. "I can only state my position and then listen to the other person's. When you commit yourself to a set of ideals, you ought to defend it without soapbox oratory, and the best way to do that is to live by what you believe.''

It was someone who lived in that way that got Wayne's eyes focused on that December wedding. "Kathy is a very special girl. I guess I'm kind of picky. I looked for certain qualities, spiritual qualities first of all, and I didn't stick around with a girl very long if she didn't have them. But as I kept dating Kathy, I liked more and more about her. I found that she had those qualities I was seeking — love, kindness, genuineness. I know she truly loves me for myself, for what I am, not in any way because I'm part of a well-known entertainment group. And that's great. That's what it's all about, after all. Although she's been in the limelight herself, all she wants to be is my wife and a mother to my children. That shows faith and confidence in me as a person. That's the kind of girl I've been looking for.''

Wayne and Kathy Osmond know each other surprisingly well and have given their lives over to each other. Their level of happiness in their mutual love is such that in a sense they have "slipped the surly bonds of earth." In time they may perhaps "reach out and touch the face of God."

"I forced Tommy to watch my mouth when I spoke. Regardless of how many times a day I would do it, I forced his little face into mine; and on many occasions, because of my anguish of heart, I would not be as gentle as I should have been. But he would always smile back at me, and this would disperse those dark clouds which hung over my shoulder." In time Olive accepted this new role of hers and pursued it with a dedicated zeal. She had made up her mind that her boy was going to talk, and to achieve this goal she became mother, teacher, clinician and companion.

When he became old enough, Tom was enrolled in the school for the deaf at Ogden, where over the years he received the concentrated and laborious effort of skilled teachers. Olive's loving, devoted and instinctively effective care was given to both Virl and Tom, and together with their own strenuous efforts this has resulted in two functioning, viable human beings who today fill an important and necessary place not only in their family but in the broader scheme of things.

Olive Osmond had to be concerned too with other matters. Following a pattern established with her first two children she made her biennial trek to the hospital for advent number three (a pattern which would vary only with Jimmy, the Omega child). Alan arrived on schedule on June 22, 1949, the child who would become the major-domo of the Osmond quartet, later quintet, later sextet, and finally septet.

Olive had a strange experience right after Alan was born. "I felt a strange euphoria, as though my spirit was leaving my body. I could hear the doctors and nurses talking, but they seemed to drift away and I couldn't get them back. The nurses were quite agitated as they talked to the doctor, and I could hear the blood-pressure pump going fast. Then I heard the doctor calling my name, but I didn't want to bother answering. It irritated me that they would disturb such a good feeling. He called louder and faster; he began to shake me. I half-heard, half-felt something. The nurses were slapping my face and rubbing my arms. Yet it was as though I was numb. I could hear the slaps, but I couldn't really feel them. I'm sure now that I had been slipping to the brink of death at that moment. That impression has stayed with me throughout the years."

George picks up the story. "I'm sure that Olive was then experiencing something we must all experience. No matter how slowly or rapidly we drift off this earth, I believe it brings home the point that there is a life after death and that this world is merely the proving ground for a greater life to come."

Around this time they both began to feel the need to improve their education. "We took some business and math courses." They bought a wire recorder; Olive would record the lessons each day, and at night George would listen to them while she did the dinner dishes. Then they would work out the answers together. This system would become a part of their family life as the boys grew and their talents developed.

Home was even happier now that there were five. One of their insurance accounts was a drive-in theater which always sent George a free family pass every year. George loved cowboy movies, and the drive-in gave him a chance to unwind after a day's work and still be with his family. So frequently they would get the kids in their pajamas, make a bed in the back of the station wagon, and take off to the movies. Virl and Tom enjoyed the cartoons at the beginning but lost interest thereafter and would soon settle down to sleep. Alan was so tiny that he slept right through it all. Olive would usually doze when the cowboys were in action. George was the only one who would endure to the end.

Children in triplicate multiplied not only permanent happiness but occasional sickness. Soon there was another dose of measles. Tom was broken out so badly that his body was one complete red rash. "He just lay in his bed and moaned. I remember sitting by his bed crying and feeling very helpless." The mumps came too, Virl, Tom, and Alan all at the same time. Olive told them stories, played games, read to them, and did everything possible to keep them quiet and in bed.

Shortly after Alan's birth, the Osmonds met a young Indian woman whose husband had deserted her. The girl needed work badly and Olive needed someone to help her, so Virginia Menard came to work for the family. In a very short time they became good friends. She loved the children and was a good worker; she would seek out things to do and never had to be directed toward work. In short order Ginny became just like one of the family. She had a talent for embroidering and Olive enjoyed sewing, so together they made several little nightgowns for the new baby's arrival. Yes, Virginia, Olive was expecting again.

On August 28, 1951, Wayne put in his appearance. Strange how every child seems so special to the mother. There's more than one reason in Wayne's case; but "with his natural baritone, we'd have been lost without him." Wayne was a quiet boy, and his fine baritone and later bass voice have provided just the right complement in the brothers' singing group. He was an interesting child. He would rarely waste time and even at an early age would be found with his head in a book or his hands engaged in some worthwhile project.

Ginny was a most attentive nurse. She took care of Olive and watched over Wayne constantly. The feeling was mutual. When Wayne started walking he'd pull on her skirt whenever he wanted something — a toy, a drink of water, or just to be picked up. "I remember she'd let him play with her red dangly rhinestone earrings," Olive recalls, "and it seemed to me he would almost swing on them. It used to make me shudder — I was afraid he'd pull her ear-lobes off."

On the west side of the house there was barely enough space to add another room, but add it they did, right to the edge of the property line. This was their schoolroom. The outside wall was just a series of windows, so that there would be plenty of light. The opposite wall was covered with blackboard paint, and a ten-foot-long chalk ledge was added. Now the boys could write or draw to their hearts' content. There was plenty of room for all. George and Olive proudly watched their boys begin to grow.

Besides Ginny there were other helpers for the mother with several small children. "I was grateful for my mother and father," Olive reminisces. "They lived across

Early cowboys, Indians, fishermen and cyclists

From
four
to
six

town, and they helped me so much. They would babysit
whenever we needed them, and often my laundry would
disappear. I knew it would be back soon, clean, folded, and
ironed ready to be put away. I don't remember Mother and
Dad ever coming to see us but what they brought a treat of
some kind in a paper sack. It was always a surprise, everything from a nice roast all cooked and ready to eat, to
cinnamon rolls, oranges, candy, or hot rolls with a pound
of butter. They have always been such kind, thoughtful
people."

Before this time Olive had acquired her real estate
license and was taking an interest in selling. One spring,
April 30, 1953, she had been out showing homes to a
"picky" little old lady. This wasn't the first time the two
had been out. "I believe I had shown her nearly every
house for sale in Ogden, and I had almost decided she just
enjoyed going for a nice ride." To Olive's surprise, the
picky little lady bought a lovely big brick home on the east
bench. Olive came home tired but rewarded and happy.
With the commission on that sale they could afford a new
roof for the house. Later in the evening certain familiar
signs let her know that it was again time to visit the
familiar haunts of the delivery room at the hospital. Several hours later Merrill became number five. "I actually
enjoyed that stay in the hospital. I was tired and I completely relaxed. I slept around the clock for a couple of
days. The nurses had to wake me up for everything —
meals, visitors, doctors, even to see the baby. After three
days of sleep I felt strong again and eager to get home."

Life was good. George and Olive were busy and
were getting along financially. They continued to improve
their home. With a new carpet and couch, they were just
putting the finishing touches on the living room when
George announced that he had found a piece of property

not far away that was just meant to be their home. They all went to look at it. It was a large red-brick house sitting on 2½ acres of land, partly orchard, and was the "best buy" in town. They bought it.

Having acquired a cow and a pasteurizer, they processed about two gallons of milk daily. George would grind wheat, and with the whole wheat flour Olive would provide that palate-tickler the family looked forward to the most — fresh homemade bread straight from the oven, with lots of butter and honey. They planted a garden, additional fruit trees, berry plants, and grape vines. They bought two more acres of ground from the neighbor to provide additional pasture for the cow.

The orchard produced abundantly and Olive took delight in canning a good share of the fruit. Perhaps it is that sensible, secure part of woman which makes her continually prepare for the future. "I can still recall the pride I felt in taking someone down to the basement to see the rows and rows of fruit I had bottled. My greatest extravagance in those days was buying jars for bottling." She loved to see things in uniform order, and those bottles of fruit were "beautiful to behold."

One year the peaches got ripe all at the same time. They saw their predicament — the peaches must be bottled in a hurry, all of them. George and the boys began to pick. Olive had expected a couple of baskets to start with and panicked when she found they had picked nine bushels. But George took over the organizing. He put the "crew" around a table and got them peeling. Olive washed the bottles, made the syrup, and processed the fruit in hot water. They had a real assembly line, a system George would later duplicate as postmaster of North Ogden. It was a tired family that went to bed that night, but the thought of two hundred quarts of peaches let them sleep easy.

Two years had gone by, so you know what's coming, don't you? Right! This was her sixth boy — March 2, 1955. Jay. The gimmick creator. The unabashed teller of shaggy-dog stories. The boy whose talent would before his nineteenth birthday earn from his peers the accolade of being noted as one of the top drummers in the world.

It was around this time that Olive first began to notice her health slipping. She tired easily and had a difficult time shaking off colds. The old "snap" seemed to have gone. She was only thirty, so age couldn't be the reason. Yet obviously something was disturbing her system. She got one infection after another. A cut on her hand which would normally heal in a day or so now took weeks to heal. Finally came another infection for which she was given massive doses of sulfa.

In her condition of deteriorating health, Olive went into the hospital for observation and possible treatment. But after running tests, the doctors indicated that they could find no reason for her illness, nor could they do anything for her. They sent her home. The day she arrived home a sense of unrest seemed to pervade her soul, an inexplicable uneasiness.

A phone at home was an extension of one in George's office, and they would both ring when a call came in. The phone rang that day and a voice asked for George. Olive recognized the voice. It was the family doctor.

Olive got George on the phone and then at an inward urging she decided to listen in. While she is one to respect the privacy of others, a doctor's call to George was almost certainly a matter of concern. Was it about her? She felt compelled to stay on the phone.

"That you, George?" came the doctor's soft voice.

"Yes, how are you, doctor?"

"George, I've got some bad news for you, and there's no sense in having you come down to my office to tell it to you."

George's guarded response and muffled reply showed the emotion of the situation. "Is it Olive?"

"George, I'm sorry. I know it's difficult to accept, but all the indications are that your wife has only about six weeks to live." The sulfa drugs had destroyed the white cells in Olive's blood.

With trembling hands Olive gently hung up the phone. When does the spectre of death become a concern of the living? Psychologists say it is somewhere around the age of forty. Even Olive's brush with death some six years before had not been allowed to detract from her zest for life. She remembered it, but did not dwell on it. This time however she felt the impact. Sitting on the edge of her bed she began to think of George with six little boys from age one to eleven. For just a brief time she became emotional and wondered, "Why me?" — the classic thought of the doomed.

She pondered the situation for a few more moments, and then got to her knees and petitioned her Heavenly Father for help. It was a simple prayer. She asked if she might be allowed to raise her boys. As the faithful will do, she conditioned her prayer with "not my will, but thine be done." When she had finished, a gentle quietus moved through her and she knew that all would be well.

Not only her family but scores of thousands of girls who were then unborn have cause to be grateful for the power of prayer and for Olive's faith in that power. For down the road, something over one year away, was Donny.

7   Merrill

It was one of those many tours with Andy Williams. Andy had taken a smaller, more rapid plane and was now several light years ahead. Filled with Osmonds, the creaking old Beechcraft rose slowly into the air; and after a few directional turns and an occasional crabbing action to compensate for the crosswinds, it settled into a deep-throated roar of appreciation at again proving its defiance of the laws of aerodynamics.

They were flying alone in heavy cloud cover when they began to hit bad weather. Their pilot, a modern-day "tailspin Tommy," was unperturbed by the bucking craft and, seeking company, called for someone to join him in the copilot's seat. It had been an exhausting day and, despite the rough weather, most of the boys had settled down to sleep. But it was more exciting to travel up front, so Merrill volunteered. He edged his way forward and climbed into the copilot's seat.

Having an inquiring mind, Merrill began to ask questions, the pilot responding with the desired information. It was slightly past midnight when he suddenly realized that he was no longer getting answers to rather leading questions such as, "What's this?" "What's that?" "What does this do?" "What would happen if I pushed this?" Merrill thought that perhaps he'd used up his quota of questions, so he settled back into his seat and fixed his gaze ahead.

When the silence became too much for him, he tried one more question. Again no reply. When he glanced toward the pilot he discovered the reason for those unanswered questions. The man at the controls was no longer at the controls. He had drifted off to the land of Nod.

Merrill watched for a few moments and then coughed loudly. He began to whistle between his teeth. He leaned over and nudged the pilot. He nudged a little harder. In an exaggerated movement he pretended to stretch and struck the sleeper smartly on the arm. All these ploys were useless. The pilot snoozed on. Over the throb of the engine Merrill heard his own exaggerated voice. "Hey! Pardon me, sir! Say! Excuse me! Aren't we up in the air?" Nothing but immobility from the man by his side.

While he pondered the situation he noticed a color change ahead. A huge black cloud was rolling toward the plane. It was rough enough riding at present, but if they went through that billowy mass with its lionheaded thunder they'd really be thrown around. The cloud got closer and Merrill made the decision. He knew that if you pushed on "the stick" the plane would go down. He pushed on "the stick." Sure enough, the plane went down — in fact the sharp dive tore the pilot from the arms of sleep. He grabbed the controls and straightened out the craft; and with a shaking voice and teeth firmly together he invited Merrill to give up the copilot's seat.

With the pilot asleep, that was one jam Merrill couldn't talk his way out of. There haven't been many such failures, for ever since grade school days his warm smile and ready words could usually be counted on to convert

Merrill Davis Osmond

the most determined adversary to friendship. He recalls though that it didn't work with a large boy in one class he was in. "I really don't know what I did to incur his displeasure, but I knew he didn't like me."

One day the boy stopped Merrill in the hall, and while his admirers watched he made the pronouncement, "Osmond, after school I'd like to beat you up." Merrill almost expected him to add, "if you don't mind," it seemed such a reticent proposal. Merrill assumed he was kidding. Giving the boy his best friendly smile, he answered in like kind: "Well, okay, it's all right with me. Sure, go ahead." Some time later he was informed that the "large boy" was quite serious and was indeed intending to "flatten him."

After school, with his books in tow, Merrill went out of the gate as usual and made his way homeward. As he glanced round he saw that "large boy" was not far behind, and further glances showed that the adversary was closing the gap. "It was getting pretty scary. It looked as if he meant business." As Merrill rounded the corner, a large hedge stood between him and the other gladiator. This was as good a place as any. He quickly set his books down and prepared for the onslaught.

He waited. He waited some more. Finally, after what seemed an interminable length of time, he peered around the corner of the hedge. "Large boy" was nowhere in sight. Merrill reasoned that good sense had finally come to the rescue, and he picked up his books and whistled his way home.

A group of Merrill's friends were known by the endearing term of "the thugs." What Merrill didn't know was that, having discovered that Merrill was in jeopardy, these boys had decided to persuade "large boy" not to bother their friend. The next day when Merrill saw his former nemesis he was shocked at his appearance. A fat lower lip, yellow discolorations around a partly closed left eye, numerous scratches on head and arms, a nose which resembled a lopsided cherry tomato. The persuasion was effective, for he gave Merrill no difficulty thereafter.

If Merrill's natural smile and happy disposition occasionally fail to get him out of a difficult situation, they stand ready always to help him into a pleasant one. Ask the former Mary Carlson, now Merrill's wife. "I was working at a summer job in a department store when a friend who was dating Alan Osmond asked me to make up a foursome as Merrill's date. I'd heard of Donny, but didn't know the names of any of the other brothers. I wasn't overly excited — the Osmonds would probably be stuck up and conceited, I thought; and although they were of my own religion, I figured that show business would have made them forget how to practice it."

"You're going out with an Osmond? How are you going to act?" That's what friends at the store asked her. "I'm just going to be myself," she replied.

And she was. What was Merrill's response? "I'd done a lot of dating, but as a rule I couldn't feel relaxed with the girls. They'd either be nervous and up-tight or snobbish, try to act sophisticated. But Mary was different, natural. I liked her from that first evening."

It was mutual — and addictive. Since Mary was tutoring Marie and Jimmy Osmond from three to five each day, Merrill found extra opportunities to see her. They spent most evenings together for six weeks or so during that June and July of 1973. There were some memorable dates — like the rocky motorcycle ride up Rock Canyon when the bike overturned at slow speed and left them both

A smile after the wedding

*A hug before
going on stage*

helpless with laughter and minus part of their pantlegs. But on many dates they would just sit and talk. "She was so easy to talk to. She was my first real friend outside the family."

Jeremy Bentham said, "True love is friendship set on fire," and Merrill and Mary would go along with this. The transition did not take long, and when the brothers' August tour was confirmed each knew that the separation would hurt. The day he arrived back, Merrill was awaiting Mary when she returned from work. The next month they were married in the Salt Lake Temple.

Sounds simple? It really wasn't. "I got a lot of resistance when it was known that I wanted to get married. I was quite young, and I was the first one of the group to be really serious about a girl. The management told me it would break up the group; and it got to the point where I just didn't know what to do." Merrill solved his problem by a lengthy prayer in the solitude of the mountains near Provo.

For Mary there was another type of problem. With a newly acquired college degree and plans to begin teaching in the coming fall, she had had innumerable job interviews in an era of teacher surpluses before finally landing a position. She had envisaged for herself a life of "hanging around Utah, teaching, and eventually getting married." After one week of teaching, she received Merrill's proposal. The next Monday she asked the school principal to release her from her contract. He did. "He was very kind. He said that if I were his own daughter he would have advised me to do just what I was doing."

Merrill's charmer from the high country of Heber City, Utah, is a delightful, pretty girl. She likes to indicate her country-girl flavor with an interesting story. "Just after we were married, the group had to perform in Las Vegas. This may make me sound like a hick, but I had never stayed in a really nice hotel, and I didn't know that in those hotels maids go in and turn the beds down. That first night in Las Vegas, when we went to our room the bed was turned down. I said, "Merrill, your brothers have short-sheeted our bed. I know they've been in here playing tricks.' I had never had room service, so it was all kind of new to a girl from the sticks."

That was the night of the famous fire in Caesar's Palace. Merrill smelled the smoke around 3:00 a.m. His first comment was, "Mary, I think you've left your electric rollers on." He finally got out of bed and gingerly opened the hall door. Grey smoke billowed in. He closed the door and in his mind began to form escape plans. He phoned the desk and was informed, "Everything is under control, just stay in your room." But under control or not, the situation didn't improve, and soon the door opened and hotel personnel, heads wrapped in wet towels, came into the room, wrapped Mary and Merrill in similar fashion, and led them to the fire escape. The fire was soon out, but not before the group had forfeited a night's sleep.

There were other surprises for Mary that first night in Las Vegas. "I didn't know Merrill played the banjo, I didn't know he tap danced, I didn't know the group played saxophones, trombones, trumpets, violins and such. All I knew was that they sang. And here they were out there dancing and playing instruments. I just had no idea that Merrill was so talented."

Merrill's brothers could have told her of other talents she wouldn't suspect, even outside of the field of entertainment. For instance, he is a natural storyteller. In earlier days, Donny, Marie and Jimmy would find a fascination about bedtime because "Merrill is gonna tell us a

Banjo-player extraordinary,
lead singer, fisherman, husband

story." Children readily sense the degree of interest in
their elders, and these three knew that Merrill enjoyed
those stories almost as much as they did. He could carry
them to faraway places, bring them to the rocking quarter-
deck of a two-masted schooner as it rounded the Cape.
Under his spell they felt the intensity of the chase as the
Pony Express rider managed to stay just ahead of the
Indians; they sensed the loneliness of Robinson Crusoe as
he stalked the island talking to himself to preserve his
sanity; they discovered the fervor and dedication of the
apostle Paul in his missionary efforts for the Christian
Church. With such stories he could at once fill the younger
minds with knowledge and delight and guide them to
dreamland.

That same voice that could charm younger brother
or sister to slumber has over the years been working its
magic on stage and recordings. For the most part Merrill
sings the lead with the group. His voice has that "quality of
strain" which is typical of today's vocalists. All the
brothers are capable of singing lead, but most of today's
singing consists of "squeezing the voice" rather than letting it flow naturally, and Merrill can "squeeze" his voice
with the best.

Merrill turns his talent for music not only to performing but also to arranging and songwriting, often in
collaboration with Wayne and Alan. Like Thomas Edison,
whose ideas sometimes seemed almost to pop out of the
air, Merrill occasionally has a tune pop into his head.
When that happens, regardless of where he is or what he's
doing, he'll try to get it down on paper or into a recorder.
One day in the shower a "great tune" came floating out of
the shower head and he needed to get it down before he
lost it. He hollered to Mary to get a tape recorder. Then,
having second thoughts, he said, "Never mind, get Donny

on the phone." He sang his creation into the phone while Donny recorded it at the studio.

Merrill's non-professional enjoyments include painting on velveteen, a technique in which the artist lays down a dozen coats of oil paint on the cloth and yet the texture of the material can still be felt. And he would have been a fine golfer if music hadn't been his first love, for he has the rhythm and fluid flow which is necessary to propel that small white ball around the fairway. As a handyman he delights in such projects as dismantling an old barn and using the wood to redecorate his den, a task he completed a year or so after marriage. Other home projects include designing bedroom and bathroom in Merrill's favorite color — black. Black walls, black rugs, black sheets and pillow cases, black towels and shower curtains — these all match Merrill's black pajamas, shirts and suits. Give him a black mask, a black hat and a sword and he could pass for Zorro.

Merrill is happy, cheerful, relaxed, positive, progressive, talented. Much involved in the business matters of the group's shows and recordings, he blocks out the staging for most of their concert shows. This man of many interests is carrying such planning skills over to his foremost interest — Mary — as together they plan their performance on life's larger stage.

8   *. . . And Three Make Nine*

George and Olive can smile now when they reflect upon the time consumed upon their early businesses. "Even though I was his secretary, I hardly ever saw him." They had turned one of their bedrooms into an office, an expedient designed to secure the best of both worlds, since George did not want Olive to leave the children with someone else. With an extension of the office phone in the bedroom, it was a busy life.

The arrival of the seventh child didn't make life any less busy, only happier. This one was Donny, an early Christmas gift the family received on December 9, 1957. There was a shared joy at the new birth, together with the other side of the coin — a little more work to be spread around. Work assignments were subject to frequent adjustment anyway as growing boys progressed to larger capabilities. While Olive looked after the home and the younger children, Virl and Tom took care of the cow and assumed a major share of the work in the garden.

Their lay-officered Church also made calls upon their time, George in particular being appointed as counselor or assistant to the bishop, the presiding officer in their local ward or congregation. This position required his services for most of Sunday and for several complete evenings a week, further reducing his time with the family. Soon he went to his bishop with a request. He would work for the Church every day of the week, around the clock if necessary, but he needed Friday nights off for family night. On Fridays the children could stay up a little later. "They thought being able to stay up late was a big deal," says Olive. "We would sing, play games, watch TV, and so on. Often George would end up carrying the children to bed one by one as they fell asleep in front of the TV. Their usual bedtime was around eight, and on Friday nights it was exceptional if they lasted past nine."

That weekly family night, which later would become the birthplace of the singing group, quickly became important to the family, and all of them looked forward to it. Olive tried to make it a special occasion for them all. There was dinner by candlelight, the children taking turns at being the master of ceremonies for the program. Sometimes they would go out. George had his usual season pass to the drive-in, so as they had done with their first three boys, now they were doing with four, five and six — on with the pj's and into the back of the station wagon. Olive would concoct a combination of popcorn, peanuts, breakfast food and pretzels, and off they'd go to fantasy land. Rarely did any of the boys make it through the entire program, and Olive usually joined them in slumber. But as it had been since the days of boys one, two and three, good old stoic George suffered through powder burns, arrows, cattle drives, burning deserts, villains defeated, maidens rescued, and all variations of the triumph of good over evil. Whatever the activity, everyone rated the evening great and eagerly looked forward to "next Friday."

Business improved. Besides working in insurance and real estate, George was appointed postmaster of North Ogden, where he began to utilize the boys in handling the mail. Olive and George's mother opened a dress shop. On Saturday the family passed out handbills, cleaned the office, and washed the car.

About this time they started the Virl fund — additional monies set aside to send the oldest boy on a two-year, full-time mission for their Church. This effort would have to be financed by the family. Virl was twelve when this fund was started, and by the time his call came to serve, the fund would be swelled by the money the boys earned in singing — sometimes five dollars a time, sometimes twenty dollars, sometimes more. (One of the choicer family anecdotes recalls the time very early in the boys' career when an emcee mentioned that their singing was financing this fund and the audience began throwing money onto the stage. Too young to know what was going on, Jay broke formation in the middle of a song and scampered hither and thither picking up the cash.)

It was that time again! After all, it was almost two years since Donny's birth, and Olive wasn't about to break the pattern. When you've got a good thing going for some fourteen years, why change? So on October 13, 1959, on George's birthday, there came into this male-oriented domain of harmony a peculiar addition — a baby girl. George was so affected by the emotion of the event that he had to take a long walk to compose himself. His first girl, after seven boys, and the special blessing of having her born on his own birthday. Now a member of a family destined for fame, Marie Osmond would in time become famous for her own talents.

That evening George went home, dressed his seven boys in similar apparel, and returned to the hospital. Here under Olive's window the older boys rendered in harmony the song, "I want a girl just like the girl that married dear old Dad.'' The serenade moved the hospital staff to tears. Olive was the only one who took it in stride.

Ernest Hemingway in one of his less defensible observations stated that the four things a man must do in his life before he has demonstrated his manhood is to plant a tree, fight a bull, write a book, and have a son. George had had seven sons, and he loved each of them with an ardor that only a parent could comprehend, yet this little brown-eyed girl was something very special to him. The new arrival had him puffed up like a pouter pigeon. Marie would bounce around the house, hang on to her mother's dress, and get generally spoiled by the boys. She had free reign to be the baby for some 3½ years. Yes! the arrival of the last child broke that "every two years" pattern. It wasn't until April 16, 1963, that Jimmy Osmond became the caboose of a very talented train.

Shortly before Marie's birth, Olive had a very impressive experience. She was in the hospital awaiting the arrival of her eighth child when she fell into a very vivid dream. She saw herself sitting by the hospital bed in a blue rocking chair when three men entered the room. "I don't remember their faces, but they were all dressed in white and the one in the middle was carrying a baby wrapped in a white blanket. He brought the infant over to me, placed it in my arms, and said in a deep, warm, resonant voice, 'This is James Arthur Osmond, one of the choicest spirits of heaven.' " Later that day when she gave birth to Marie she asked the doctor three times in one hour, "Are you sure it's a girl?" It was only after the baby was placed in her arms and she saw the unmistakable features of the Osmond clan, that she was sure this was her little girl and there hadn't been some mixup of babies.

Later when George came to see her she told him

Marie and Jimmy "doing what comes naturally"

The only girl

The Omega child

about the dream. "There's one more out there for us, George, and I won't rest until we have him in our home." Finally Jimmy came. Olive could rest.

One of the things which has made this family so tight-knit is that they have always done things together. Over-familiarity can occasionally lead into a contempt factor, but in this family the effect was the opposite — it "brought us closer together." They worked as a team. Neither parent ever felt that his work or her work was below the other's dignity. George serviced about seventy accounts for the radio station, sold real estate and insurance, and was busy shaping the boys' careers. "There is no way I could have done it without Olive. She was the best bookkeeper, secretary, accountant, manager, hostess, housekeeper, wife and mother a man could ask for. She was never too busy or too tired to help me with something."

Free time was scarce, and the boys now agree that that was one of the advantages of being raised in this family. There were always projects going. Each of them had something he was responsible for. Milking the cow, feeding the chickens, weeding the garden, churning the butter, watering, shoveling, irrigating, painting, and the post office. After the chores there were three hours of music, singing, and instruments. This was the pattern five days a week. They learned to pull together, and in their case pulling together has pulled them together.

Their post office operation involved the same Osmondology. Although they were in North Ogden, when people found out how efficiently their substation worked, especially around Christmas time, they would make the trip across town to connect their letters with that "fast-moving line." Alan remembers the fun of going to the post office after school to build his own mountain of mail.

George and the boys – family project

George and
Olive –
family
progenitors

The boys have always enjoyed the challenge to excel, and although each tried to outdo the other, when one reached his own personal zenith the others cheered for him. Merrill took banjo lessons and came home to teach the rest. Virl and Tom learned to tap dance and taught the rest. Olive taught them the saxophone. Wayne taught them the woodwind and drums. Alan taught them the trumpet. Similarly with other instruments. They all picked up the trombone. There wasn't enough money for lessons for all of them in all the various instruments, but by interteaching they have mastered sixteen instruments between them and have done it while each has maintained his own individual sense of balance.

A large family in particular needs means of maintaining order and motivating the children, so at one time this family used a merit and demerit system. If someone failed to do his chores, didn't hang up his clothes, let his school grades decline, or in general didn't measure up, he was stuck with demerits; and when these were totaled up on Monday the one with more than a certain number of demerits would be assigned extra work. Merrill usually wore the goat horns, and later Jay came in for his share of the booby prizes. Merrill and Jay washed a lot of dishes, folded an army of clothes, and packed out a ton of garbage. It hasn't seemed to harm them at all, even to hamper their natural vivacity. As a matter of fact, both Merrill and Jay have a highly developed sense of humor.

Under the system, the one with the least demerits and the most merits likewise received his reward. With that in mind, when the list of chores was posted they would vie with each other to do the more difficult ones because those carried the highest number of merits. At the Friday family night the highest achiever would be presented with a little prize, which Olive had wrapped in

Togetherness is . . .

fancy paper and tied with a bow. To the growing boys this became a very coveted and prestigious award.

Deliberately the Osmonds have kept their lives uncomplicated. Olive and George passed up most outside activities to be with their children, and in their mature years those children are conscious of this and in turn keep their own lives simplified. Olive reflects: "We were thrilled with each of our nine babies. We always felt they were extra special and that the good Lord required us to do our very best with each of them. I don't remember a time when we ever wanted to be away from them. I recall one night some friends of ours came to the house and said, 'Let's pawn the kids off on Grandma next week and take a trip to Yellowstone Park.' We knew that Yellowstone Park would be a pleasure to visit, and we enjoyed these friends, so George and I talked it over. I can remember what he said almost immediately: 'If I can't take the kids with me, I don't want to go.' That was that, and that's how it's always been with this family."

This "togetherness" attitude has rubbed off on their stage appearances. The brothers are extremely conscious of fan attitude and realize that fan apathy would mean the eventual demise of the group. Apart from that, they have a warmth about them that makes them want to perform to please their fans. But they have another, longer-term motivator. When it's time to go on stage, it's "OK, guys, let's go out there and make Father happy." In the early days it was always Father who traveled with the boys; it was Father who critiqued the group; it was Father who sat out front and took notes or who stood behind the curtains and performed the entire routine in time with the boys on stage. If they did a bad show, it was Father who corrected them. It was Father who usually spotted a weakness and shored up the foundation. It was Father who took care of their needs as they traveled, encouraged them before and after a show, saw that they got to bed, calmed them with a story before they went to sleep, and arranged the innumerable details of life on the road. It's quite a while ago, but the boys don't forget. Now, as then, they still want to go out there and "make Father happy."

And they do. But to do so they know that they must keep improving, which in turn means they must know which areas need improvement, even what they are doing wrong. They are not afraid of criticism and are willing to listen to anyone who can be constructive. But again it falls mostly to George Osmond to give that kind of help. "He knows us so well," says Wayne, "and it's hard when he's not around, because it's difficult trying to relate to someone else telling us what's wrong. Father will not pussyfoot with us, and we appreciate that. When he's not around, there's a danger that we'll let down a little, but when he's back with us we're right on top again."

On top again. That's where their parents have trained them to be. On or off the stage, they're still making Father (and Mother) happy.

9   *Jay*

There are those famous people who have the super-star attitude of sitting back, a bit aloof, waiting for the clamoring public to force its attention upon them, and then in the spirit of reticence giving grudgingly of themselves. Jay Osmond is just the reverse — outgoing, friendly with everyone he meets. He extends his right hand, walks toward the person, and says "Hi! I'm Jay Osmond." He has none of the phony "I-know-you're-delighted-to-meet-me,-but-would-you-please-buzz-off," attitude. It's "Hi, Jim!" "Hi, George!" "Hi Paul!" When he knows your name he uses it.

Jay is the court jester of this royal family of music. The beneficiaries of his humor enjoy the effort Jay goes through to set up a prank or to deliver a joke — especially the punch line. The listeners enjoy Jay's jokes almost as much as he does. You know when the punch line is coming because in anticipation of it his wide grin is staccatoed with laughs; then, just before delivering the punch line, it becomes an all-out guffaw. As he's joined in appreciation by those upon whose ears those nuggets of humor have fallen, his feel for the humor of a situation is such that, what with the joke itself and the listeners' reaction, his laugh rises and rings with the others and sustains itself until theirs are echoes.

Olive and George credit Jay with the gimmick which broke them into show business. When they first started performing for television, the boys were told to follow the camera which had the red light glowing. When moving from one camera to another they were to make it a slow and natural transition; not to act as if they had been singing to one part of the audience and then had suddenly transferred their attention to another section, but to make the change in a smooth, fluid motion. "Watch the red light on the camera, kids, and when it goes off and comes on another camera, that's the camera you're on. Just make a natural turn into that camera."

At six years of age Jay wasn't too sure about natural turns and smooth fluid motions, but he did know that the camera was "hot" when the light came on. Clearly it was best to get on that camera as quickly as possible. So while Alan, Wayne and Merrill made that smooth move toward the camera when it called for a change, Jay moved with all the fluid motion of an old-vintage movie — rather like an animated Charlie Chaplin. Nature having enhanced the effect in the way she is prone to do with six-year-olds, Jay's middle four teeth on the top side were missing, and with his bright open smile he captured hearts in thousands of households. The cameramen of course became conscious of what was going on, so they switched cameras somewhat more than necessity demanded. In this way Jay's face, with his beautiful gapping smile, was always on camera. While his brothers were making that nonchalant turn into the camera, Jay was already there — and preparing for the next move. He became so good at it that he could anticipate the move; so regardless of how fast it occurred, there was Jay hamming it up and sliding over his S's as he hissed his way through a song.

Thousands of letters proved that people wanted to

Jay Wesley Osmond

see more of this kid with no teeth and an eye for the camera. Needless to say, when the American public found out the innate talent of these boys, no gimmicks were needed.

While all of the group are good natural athletes and fleet of foot, Jay is probably the best all-around athlete and dancer among them. He assists Merrill, from whom he learned the choreographer's skill, to choreograph the brothers' onstage moves, yet Jay still has found time to earn the acclaim of his peers in that field as an exceptional drummer. Continuing the family tradition, like Marie and Jimmy he takes music lessons. At time of writing he's learning the piano and his teacher is his younger brother Donny, an accomplished pianist in his own right.

Jay has not always been Mr. Graceful, for there was a time when, to use his own words, he "had difficulty in chewing gum and walking at the same time." He has the scars to prove his proneness to falling off things — chairs, stools, bicycles, almost anything. One of the earliest incidents, over which his control was minimal, took place on (or we might say *off*) a horse which George had bought for the family to ride, a pinto whose sluggish qualities had earned it the name of Flash. On first acquaintance, Jay like all the others yearned to feel that horseflesh beneath him, to sense the power of controlling that noble animal as it bore him swiftly over field and hedge. But these burning desires were hampered by one small detail — being very young, he was afraid to get on the horse.

Olive remedied this situation by mounting the horse and holding Jay in front of her. No problem. But it was just about now that Merrill, anxious to give an appropriate welcome to this new addition to the family, produced a carrot. Flash must have been a member of the horses' union, for apparently he objected to working while he was

Basketball pointers given during a practice game with Donny and Jimmy

A long way from the pan and the spoons

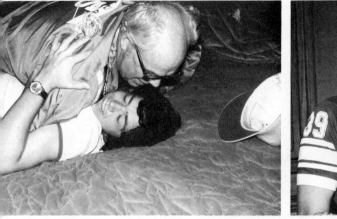

*It's all in fun —
wrestling with
Father, playing with
a nephew, jogging
down the lane*

eating; and he reared up and slid his riders off. Jay landed on top of his mother.

There were worse places to land, Jay discovered. Once in the early seventies, in an effort to impress a doe-eyed damsel, he came down a forty-five-degree hill on a bicycle. He was clad only in swimming trunks at the time. Standing at the bottom of the hill and using her most alluring tones, the damsel said, "Come on, Jay!" It was the signal for the daredevil to descend "Widow-maker."

Down he started, that ever-present grin suffusing his countenance. Halfway down he thought he'd better just test his right brake. He squeezed it, and a cold hand squeezed his chest — the lever came all the way back to the handlebar and the bike seemed to gain speed. The grin disappeared, to flick back on again when he remembered that his bike had two brakes and he hadn't even tried the other one yet. As he neared the bottom at something approaching "mach one" speed, he clamped hopefully on that left brake. It was as effective as the right one had been. He was hurtling downhill on a brakeless bike. He remembers that as he shot past his girl friend they didn't even exchange any pleasantries, and shortly after passing her he broke the sound barrier.

Jay's thoughts now were principally on the intersection which loomed ahead. "I could either lay it down or somehow try to get through that intersection." He had about one-half of a second to make the decision. He "laid the bike down." Too bad that he had to lay himself down with it, because his scanty attire insured that he erased part of himself in the process. Shoulders, back, legs, arms and sundry portions of the body witnessed to the unfairness of any contest between epidermis and asphalt.

Jay slid between several cars and came to rest in the

center of the intersection. Dazed and shaken he stood up, tried a grin, managed a weak one, looked apologetically at the cars, placed a battered arm over the shoulder of the doe-eyed damsel, and hobbled off to the hospital.

There were other brushes with the inelegant. Several years earlier, while receiving a haircut on a four-legged stool, he thought he'd try to find out what it was like to fall backwards. It was like a broken collarbone. (So that Jay wouldn't feel unique, Donny repeated this inept feat one year later from the same stool under the same circumstances and achieved the same results, a broken collarbone on the same side as Jay's.)

On a tour some years ago, in a water fight Jay ducked to avoid a stream from Merrill's paper cup. He shouldn't have been so averse to water. His skull came into quick contact with a washbasin, and he wound up with a big cut over the eye and enough stitches to require the services of one large cat. Performing a karate routine with his brothers on stage, his nose accidentally came into contact with Alan's right hand and the bone was broken in several places. Just to prove it wasn't a feat he couldn't repeat, he rebroke the bone two weeks later in a game of pass and touch with his beloved football. When you watch this young man move in a dance routine or observe the intricate coordination he has with sticks, cymbals, bells, tom-toms, snare, and bass, you're grateful that he has survived long enough to become one of the top drummers in the business.

Jay has enough athletic talent and football savvy to play in college, and were it not for traveling with the group he might have made his name in the athletic world. In a golf tournament for celebrities and professionals alike he shot in the upper 90's after only two months at the game. (Since only 20 percent of the golfing public ever legitimately break 100, he made giant strides in those two months.) He enjoys the company of girls and loves to date, but like his brothers before him he is selective. He is great fun on a date, where with a girl he can enjoy skiing (water or snow), horseback riding, tennis, hiking, golf, or mountain climbing.

Jay's sense of humor and easy attitude belie the seriousness behind those brown eyes. Successful men the world over follow the same plan for achieving: Rise early, program your day, and set about accomplishing what you have planned. That is how Jay works. He rises early, reads a chapter in the scriptures, exercises vigorously for fifteen minutes, takes a shower, eats breakfast. Then he begins on those things he has programmed for the day. "If for some reason or other I don't accomplish all I set out to do, the day is not as satisfying as it should be, and it spurs me on to do better tomorrow. I believe you need goals to achieve satisfaction and success. And I believe you must not set those goals too low. If a person ever achieves all he set out to do, somehow he's moved past striving and must either reevaluate his position or retire."

That doesn't sound much like the court jester. It sounds more like the king himself. That is fitting, for where truth, progress and happiness are concerned, this young man is of a royal lineage.

10   *Look Back and Laugh*

The world of entertainment does not consist solely of rehearsing, setting up equipment, performing, escaping the clutches of over-excited fans, taking meals in hotel rooms, and then going wearily to bed with the assurance of facing the same routine tomorrow. Fortunately there are splashes of the unexpected, even of humor.

One early-day incident was repeated sufficiently to be no longer unexpected but always humorous. In those days they were doing shows at the Hotel Utah in Salt Lake City and commuting from Ogden back and forth every night. To make it on time for their performance, George frequently had to be a little heavy on the gas pedal, and it was not uncommon for policemen along the route to take exception to this. They would pull the car over and ask to see George's license. As he handed it over, George would say, "My boys here are the Osmond Brothers, and we're just on our way to a performance and we're late." He'd ask, "Would you like to hear them sing?" Then the boys would belt out a song. They don't recall ever getting a ticket on those trips.

Old troupers like the Osmonds have learned to expect the unexpected and to handle it with whatever grace is possible. All the same, after one particular experience they'd prefer not to have to follow an elephant act again. That July night in Reno, Nevada, some of these behemoths had been pirouetting, each on one drum-shaped foot, and performing other pachydermal prodigies before a whistling and applauding audience while the Osmond brothers awaited their turn. Finally the elephants ambled off stage to their reward. But since elephants don't have to conform to the mores of Homo sapiens, during such acts there's bound to be the occasional "accident," and this was one of those nights.

So it was that after Bertha and Tina the performing pachyderms had vacated the stage, the spotlight went out, a drum roll resounded, and the emcee's voice came on: "And now, ladies and gentlemen, the Osmonds." Introductory music. The spotlight came back on and focused on Alan's spot on the stage — and right there was a spot which Bertha or Tina had inadvertently left. Both the audience and the boys were quick to perceive the problem, but it was the performers who must find the solution. It seemed to come with complete naturalness as Alan looked down, glanced around him, then smiled out into the audience and asked, "Does anyone have a shovel?" With the offending spot removed, the Reno audience, which had always been receptive to these boys, outdid themselves that night.

Many an audience have outdone themselves in a different way, for fans are always trying to get the group's attention during a performance. It is not uncommon for fans to throw flash cubes at the performers; as a matter of fact, Marie was hit on the body and neck by several of these missiles in one of the first concerts she performed with the group. Donny has had the same welcome. Again, since apparently each fan feels that the group is performing for her and her alone, they loft little gifts through the air in the

*Fans await
the Osmonds'
appearance*

Donny sings to delighted listener

direction of the stage — pennies, jelly beans, pens and pencils, wallets, shoes and other miscellaneous apparel.

This kind of thing is all the more disconcerting since those on stage can't see the objects until they suddenly emerge from the darkened hall onto the lighted stage. One night, on the state fair circuit, a large black object loomed out of the lights. "At first I thought it was a snake with a rather large head, but as it whistled by me and buried itself in my amplifier, I saw it was a pair of binoculars. I really wondered if someone was wanting me to retrieve those glasses and by some magic spot the thrower in a crowd of seventeen thousand." Wayne's observation was more correct than he imagined. Fans do relate on a one-to-one basis.

That one-to-one can become a closer reality off stage, for like many another performer the Osmonds have been engulfed in tidal waves of fans, buffeted by the screams of approval, even stripped of items of clothing. This inexplicable phenomenon of fan hysteria will even impel an ardent admirer to inflict physical violence on her favorite. Caught in a milling crowd of fans in England when the family returned to their hotel after a shopping spree, Jay found himself in the bulldog-like grip of one young charmer who in the confusion had managed to get a stranglehold on his neck from behind. Regardless of the growing hues of red and blue which painted Jay's face, and ignoring his gasps for air, she hung on with a tenacity that would have brought approval from a student of the Greco-Roman style of wrestling. Like his brothers, Jay is too much of a gentleman ever to strike a lady, yet in his position this was about the only option open to him if he still cared about survival. Fortunately his mother had seen his plight, and struggling through the human mass she managed to reach him, grab one of the girl's arms, and exert enough physical pressure to bring about the vital disengagement.

Most of the brothers have had their close calls in the battle of wits between determined fans and safety-seeking performers. In an escape attempt one night, Alan bolted headlong into an iron girder. The girder won. He began to leak crimson and the surging tide did not look like abating. He sprang to his feet, took a few wobbly steps, and then gained speed as he headed for the dubious protection of a limousine. Apparently he wasn't functioning on all cylinders, because as he viewed the car's open door and made that rapid ducking move to enter, he somehow forgot about the guitar which dangled horizontally around his waist. The crunch and the deceleration together told him he had totalled out a five-hundred-dollar electric guitar.

Security arrangements can easily fail in the presence of the unexpected, as an Ohio State Fair engagement showed. In an attempt to make the usual fast escape after a show, the brothers ran all the way to the limousine and jumped in it and the driver pulled away. The boys sighed with relief and waved back at the pursuing teen-agers as the car made for the gate — the only gate a car could exit by. Their sense of security was short-lived, for by a remarkable feat of timing, when they reached the gate a perverse fate was just bringing through it towards them one of the world's most undeflectable objects — a large marching band! Consternation! Policemen shouting and waving their arms to get the band out of the way. Trumpets giving an "uncertain sound," as instruments were jostled in the crush. Raucous noises from other brass. Several different beats going, as drummers struggled to recover an already lost situation. And the impeccable columns and rows finally breaking up into a straggling mass of feet, arms, and glistening brass.

Meanwhile another straggling mass was at work, the surging horde of teen-agers now having caught up

In cowboy garb, one costume of years back

In leis, on leaving Hawaii

with the stranded limousine. Unable to get to its occupants, they beat their fists on the car, pushed against it, climbed on top of it. When it was able to move, several valiant ones still clung to it like leeches. And six blocks down the road the driver finally stopped to let the last three or four climb down in safety from the top of the car, where they stood in the road waving at the Osmonds until the vehicle passed from view.

George has found that neither age nor non-performing status are any guarantee, that frustrated young females will attack any object if it's an Osmond. After being thwarted in a surge to encompass the performers one hot Saturday afternoon, the fans began milling around the now-vacant stage. In their necessarily rapid exit the boys had left pieces of equipment on stage, and George, subconsciously assuming himself to be immune from the fans' attentions, now went back to the stage and began to dismantle the props. He looked towards the girls as they noticed him, and in his warm and friendly way he said, "Hi, girls!" as he raised his right hand in a wave. "Half a league, half a league, half a league onward,/Into the valley of death rode the six hundred." This time the six hundred were surging out of a valley up onto the stage and riding straight for George. George has an above-average I.Q. and it didn't take him long to realize that the screams, the squeals and the thundering feet would soon engulf him and that, notwithstanding the vicarious nature of his current action, he stood in physical jeopardy. He gained the awe and respect of his entire family when he reached down for the sprinter's speed, snatched up a portion of it, and outdistanced the pursuing horde to make his getaway.

There are those among the Osmonds who know something of how a fan can feel, having themselves been on the other side of the security arrangements. After a show they gave in London, the brothers were to leave under police protection in a paddy wagon, and somehow that time Alan was running a few steps behind the others. With the London bobbies straining to hold back the human waves, inevitably there were a few breakthroughs. When Alan reached the wagon, the rest of the group having dived into it seconds before, in the darkness Alan looked like a breakthrough to the policemen, who were already in the act of closing the door. A couple of them accordingly pounced upon him and unceremoniously threw him back into the crowd. Only the frantic explanations of the wagon occupants saved Alan from who knows what fate. Ever after that he has felt a great empathy with those who anciently were thrown to the lions.

Olive's experience was more embarrassing than dangerous. The group was performing in Birmingham, Alabama, when Olive left the dressingroom accompanied by Marie, and with a tape recorder strung across her shoulder walked out into the audience to record from that position a portion of the show and the audience reaction. The show over, she watched the boys leave the stage and take off in the limousine; then as the crowd began to disperse, she and Marie went back to get their purses from the dressingroom. But now there was a barrier up, and when they broke through it they were stopped by a big colored policeman.

Obviously these two were a fan and her mother. "Where do you think you're going, Ma'am?"

"I'm going backstage."

"Well, you're not!" There was an air of finality about his reply.

"I'm the mother of the Osmond brothers, and . . ."

"That's what they all say." A slight pause. "Can you show me some identification?"

"I can if you'll let me past. My purse is in the dressingroom."

Skepticism and unbelief mounted. "If you were their mother you'd be in the limousine with them. You're not going back there."

Argument would clearly be of no avail, so Olive tried to reason with him, while the tape recorder took it all down. At last he offered to get the stage manager. "We'll see if you're the mother of the Osmonds."

If they could just get backstage there would be no problem, so while the policemen went to see the stage manager Olive and Marie sneaked past the barrier and made their way toward the backstage area. But no luck! The policeman came back too soon and caught them half-way — and was he mad!

Moments later the stage manager appeared. "Do you know this lady?" the policeman asked. The man looked, frowned, shook his head, "I never saw her before in my life." Olive began to wonder what she'd done to deserve all this.

The barrier and the policeman remained adamant for some time, but finally a member of one of the acts in the show came into view. He could see Olive was in difficulty, and he called out, "Hey, that's Mrs. Osmond!" The embarrassment was now on the other side — and much deeper. For the remainder of the engagement the policeman was noticeably hanging his head.

But Olive is compassionate and understanding. On the last night, with the show over and everyone gathered on stage talking, she made a little speech. "Could I have your attention for a minute. There's something I'd like to say." She asked the policeman to come over to her — which he did with some apparent trepidation. Then she said: "I just want to compliment this policeman. When I can't get through the barriers myself, I know my kids are being protected; and I just want you all to know that I appreciate this man for doing such a fine job."

With this kind of problem in mind, the family now are frequently issued identifying buttons so that they can get backstage at shows. Merrill's wife Mary may be excused if she is not convinced of their effectiveness. Wearing the button on her collar at Madison Square Garden, she was sitting at the side of the stage watching the brothers perform when a guard spotted her. She must be a fan who had somehow got through the large barriers out there in front of the stage. As such she was guilty until proved innocent — and she'd better not expect a chance to prove her innocence. Without more ado, the guard picked Mary up and walked away, with the clear intention of disposing of her on the other side of the barrier.

Mary had other ideas about it, but her screamed explanations merely added an insignificant irritant to the higher-decibeled sounds assailing the guard's ears from the stage and served no purpose as a means of communication. In desperation, and at the risk of dislocating a shoulder, Mary finally managed to yank clear the arm on which side the identifying button was pinned and to thrust it into the line of vision of the otherwise impervious guard. In a superb vindication of the teaching concept that one picture is worth a thousand words, schoolteacher Mary thus managed to secure her immediate release and her unmolested enjoyment of the remainder of the show.

Since Donny is more often than not the major object of the fan mania, he has occasionally been used as a decoy.

He has stood on balconies, landings, and parapets above the madding crowd and waved to them while his brothers were ducking out the back way. On one occasion, on leaving the British Broadcasting Corporation in London, their escape route lay along a line of back yards complete with fences or walls to scale. The strategy called for them to surface at a Chinese restaurant, where by prearrangement they would go through the kitchen and out the front door to a waiting, predesignated taxi. Donny would catch up with them in the restaurant.

All went as planned till the brothers were halfway through the Chinese restaurant, when the crowd suddenly surged in front on the street and the sidewalk. Instantly the brothers all dived for the floor. Observing them in their horizontal positions, the reserved English diners continued their meal, wondering perhaps at the unusual happening but not wishing to interfere in the business of the obviously deranged Americans.

The crowd passed, and the boys stood up and moved quickly toward the waiting taxi. Inside quickly! Lock the door! Too late — they had been discovered! Out into the traffic the driver urged his taxi, while scores of fans followed on their bicycles. After a mile or so the driver had shaken off the pursuers and the boys settled back in relief to await delivery at their next appointment.

They were in trouble about that appointment, which was only one hour ahead. In lunging into the taxi outside the restaurant, they had been more concerned about the predatory look on their fans' faces than about the surprised look on the taxi-driver's face. While prearrangements had been made for a taxi to be at a specific spot at a specific time, they now discovered that the taxi they were in was not that taxi. The appointed taxi had been hung up in the pandemonium around the BBC, and the driver had missed connections. This situation presented a problem. The appointed taxi-driver knew where the Osmonds were to perform next, but the present driver did not and nor did the boys. It took some time to straighten this one out, but they managed to make it to the next appointment. Today only the humorous parts of the incident remain a memory.

It was a taxi ride that brought them a wholly humorous situation. One spring day on their way from a performance the boys and George were in a taxi on their way to the airport. As the conversation progressed, the driver heard the boys repeatedly address the older man as "Father." What he didn't know is that while many youngsters call their father Dad or some other affectionate diminutive, these boys have always called George *Father* — not as a formal thing, but as the pattern they've adopted.

The talk continued. "How did it really go, Father?" "Father, did you like that new dance step we used?" "Are we going to eat at the airport or on the plane?" "I don't know; ask Father." As they got out of the cab at the airport, Wayne said, "Father's going to take care of the fare." Then as George paid him, the cabbie tipped his hat, looked at George with something of reverence in his eyes, and said, "Thank you, Father."

"I didn't want to embarrass him by telling him the truth — that I was not a Catholic priest but the boys' father," says George. "He was obviously a Catholic himself, by the things he was saying, and he kept me chatting there for a few minutes. I knew the boys were cracking up inside, and it was as much as I could do to keep a straight face until he got in his cab and drove away."

The family "rap" sessions bring out plenty of humorous recollections of both offstage and onstage ac-

Barbershop days —
original, and revisited
for fun

tivities. There was Wayne in the early days, cinching up his suspenders so tightly that they pulled him upright to his tiptoes and made him walk so rigidly that George called him the robot. There was Donny, who enjoyed swallowing things like buttons and coins and was kissed early in life by a 120-volt wall socket when he decided to investigate the source of electricity. Jay would manage to fall off anything higher than the floor. Alan fell off the end of a stage, to be found some time later groping around in the dark.

For Merrill there was the classic occasion when the group was performing on stage using steps as risers. One of the lines of the song was, "High is better than low." With the boys dancing their way higher, Merrill was on the top tier when his part of the temporary stairs broke. He plunged downward, grabbed a portion of the stair before he struck the stage, and dangled there. Now, instead of ten dancing feet going "higher," there were eight dancing feet going "higher" and two dancing hands going "lower."

Going lower was the name of the game when, on a brief vacation in the Bahamas, the boys decided they wanted to learn how to scuba dive. They took a three-day crash course, on the final day of which they were to go out in the ocean to the fifteen-foot depth and practice what they had been taught. Because of high winds and a running surf the visibility at fifteen feet was nil, so the instructor decided to move them out to the forty-foot depth. The water looked clear, and the boys one by one jumped into the rolling sea.

Jay immediately lost his weight belt and could only kick and splash topside until his instructor retrieved it. Alan was gripped by motion sickness and tried to combat the nausea while bouncing on six- to ten-foot swells. He finally gave up for the time being and clambered back in the boat. Meanwhile, Jay, Donny, Merrill and Wayne had gone under water, where the effects of the sea's motion are lessened. Down there, drawing on their experience with their two oldest brothers, they communicated with each other in sign language.

After a while Alan felt a little better and decided to submerge and join the group. Down below he mistook the begoggled instructor for Jay and began to talk to him in sign language. The instructor just shrugged his shoulders and, failing to comprehend, ignored the signals. This wouldn't do for Alan, so to emphasize his point and secure an answer from the supposed Jay he grabbed the instructor by the hair and began shaking him. As soon as he could extricate himself the instructor quickly shot topside. He carefully avoided Alan for the remainder of the dive. Even on shore later he watched Alan with a quizzical eye.

11   Donny

A motor whirrs, and the bed rises to reveal a workbench. A switch is touched, a door in the ceiling opens, and a clothes closet descends. If he wishes, the occupant can ascend on the bed through another ceiling door, close it behind him, and revel in his absolute privacy. He can take his bookshelf up with him or leave it on the mundane floor level. Similarly, with his electric motors, ropes, and pulleys, he can move all of his furniture out of his room except the work bench.

A movie set mock-up for one of the more exotic movies? A fantasy from the pages of *NineteenEighty-Four*? Neither. It's just Donny Osmond's "everyday" bedroom. And he engineered and wired it himself.

Like his brothers, Donny does not confine his interests to the major one of music and related topics. Even without his talents in that area he could have made a respectable living in electronics, a field in which he was initially taught by Alan and particularly by Wayne. With their help and by a self-teaching process he has gained considerable knowledge of such esoteric matters as ohms, watts, amperes, volts, joules, input, output, A.C. and D.C., plus an aptitude which allows him to put such knowledge to practical use. "I really don't know when I caught the bug," he says. "I think it was about the age of three, when I put my forefinger in a hot plug."

The development of this skill didn't come without a lot of interesting incidents. In the process he has cut into a fair number of hot wires, forgot to turn circuits off when wiring, shorted out whole buildings. But he's got a lot to show for it. One Christmas the family gave him the components of a color television set to put together. He did. It works. Then there's the elegant lighting fixture on the Osmonds' living-room ceiling, a circle (to represent the family name) five feet in diameter whose thirty-two circumference lights are reflected by the similar-dimensioned mirror above it. Better than that, before he was seventeen he had designed, developed and wired the electrical and electronic features of the family's professional recording studio. He set up the mike system, equalized the lighting, balanced the ends, inserted four-, eight-, sixteen-, and twenty-four-track recorders. Even before that was completed he was already planning some other highly creative projects.

Donny enjoys all the wrong foods — tacos, spaghetti, biscuits with creamed tuna, macaroni — yet he remains delightfully thin. "I burn it all up in the studio." During his waking hours Donny can usually be found doing some project in the recording studio. He's given carte blanche with these projects because of his obvious genius for electronics and because he focuses on the improvement of existing conditions.

As well as being the electronics expert in the dream studio, Donny serves as the resident engineer. When he is not recording or performing he is frequently to be found at the control panel, where he will be checking for "level," mixing the blend, and so on. He finds it is quite feasible to do this on his own behalf, for when he rerecorded a song

Donald Clark Osmond

he was not pleased with, he set the mike next to the board and began to sing, overdubbing it and recording it at the same time. It turned out well.

"It's a lot more fun to sing with a girl than it is with my brothers." This was Donny's answer to a query about singing with Marie. He and Marie have always been close. Donny wasn't quite two years old when Marie broke up the pattern and became the first girl after fourteen years of boys. They played together as young children, and until both were of school age Donny had no interest in becoming another singing Osmond. He was generally more interested in such activities as the application of peanut butter to door knobs, dressers, clothing, and anything within reach. He even enjoyed smearing up himself and his sister. One afternoon Donny and Marie painted the interior of the house with a five-pound can of the gooey paste.

From those early years Donny recalls one of the brisk, soft days of Utah's winter when snow fell in abundance. It would be such fun, he concluded, for him and Marie to launch snowballs over Grandma's hedge, as they often did in winter, even though they'd probably have to content themselves with one strike in ten. After a series of failures that day they finally had the timing, the elevation, and the trajectory lined up and they hurtled one that landed on the windshield of a passing car.

Their glee at their success was quickly turned to terror as flashing red and blue lights appeared on the roof of the vehicle and it turned 180 degrees and started back toward them. They'd hit a police car. Their retreat cut off by the length of open ground separating them from the house, they tried to lie down behind the hedge, but to no avail. An officer of the law, who was probably ten or twelve feet tall, appeared over the crouched forms; and

Press a button, and up goes Donny's bed

Press another,
and down comes a
clothes closet

Press still another,
and the bed area is concealed

At the piano

Writing a lyric

Relaxing with
an electronics manual

between sobs they caught a few of the reasons for retiring from the projectile business.

"It was neat to turn nine on the ninth." (Donny realizes that to the age of 31, everyone who was not born on February 29 has a day when the numbers of the date and his birthday fall together.) On that ninth birthday he received a purple Stingray bike. "That was the neatest thing I ever saw in my life." That's when he became enamored with that particular part of the color spectrum.

Colors! Each of the brothers has adopted a color as his own, and these have been their trademark throughout the years — blue, yellow, black, green, purple and red. In thousands of American homes, parents wonder about the purple drapes in their daughter's bedrooms, purple linen, purple rugs, purple teddy bears, purple fingernail polish, purple shoes and wearing apparel. If they were to watch Donny on stage with his wide-collared purple shirt, open at the neck, his white suit dressed with a purple handkerchief flowing from the breast pocket, his purple belt, his purple buttons, and if they were to watch their daughters' faces as he cavorts behind the footlights, it wouldn't be all that difficult to put two and two together. This penchant for purple is one way girls show they like Donny. How does he feel about girls?

"I really do like girls," Donny admits. He has always wanted to take a girl to the ranch for an all-day date. "Get to the ranch early, have breakfast, and then go horseback riding through the beautiful Wasatch range. Get back to the ranch for lunch, and then take off for an afternoon of boating and water skiing." He feels that a good ending to a day like that would be a nice leisurely dinner at one of the supper clubs, and then a movie. "Someday I'm gonna do that." He shouldn't have too many problems getting a date.

It's no secret to him that he has good looks. The thousands of letters addressed to him every week would be reminder enough that he is blessed in this area. But while thousands of girls might dream of marrying Donny Osmond, he has his own ideas of what his wife will be like. "I think I would look for the spiritual aspect." When nudged further, he admits that boys do look at the physical first. "That's what confronts them, of course. But you can only look so long, and soon there's a desire to communicate one on one. It doesn't take long to find out what's up, and before the conversation has gone very far you know a great deal about that person." In short, while Donny is normal in recognizing the significance of physical beauty in a girl, there are other qualities more important to this young man.

"Family background is important, for instance, but if a girl comes from a broken home she certainly can't be faulted for that. She might even have a deeper appreciation for good family ties than the average."

More has been written about Donny Osmond than any other member of the family. Are his talents such that they surpass those of his brothers? No, and he would be the first to tell you so. Yet while his talents, like theirs, are considerable, he stands in the position of having grown up with his fans. He has been in the public eye most of his life; yet the unusual combination of fame and youthful growth have left him singularly unaffected. He seems to have slipped past that awkward age which mires down many youngsters during puberty. The transition went smoothly for him and with very few hitches.

Like the rest of the entertaining family, Donny is conscious of his appearance and grooming. Naturally this all enhances his appeal to the fans. Girls squeal at his

. . . personally

"Come and help me, help me, pl-ea-se." When he croons
that line, they all have the answer to Donny's plea —
themselves. Infinitely different as individuals, they are
alike in that single-minded conviction that each is herself
the answer to the plaintive cry of the opposite gender. That
cry awakens the maternal part of girls but is quickly transferred to the romantic. What does this all do to Donny?
He's very sane and balanced about it. He enjoys the trappings of the star, but he ages with his success in an adult
manner. Like his brothers, he's a polished, self-confident
performer and has that innate quality of knowing just how
to "milk" an audience. His charisma exudes past his own
peers out into the adult audience.

Donny is the first to recognize that his performing
skills result from family help and encouragement, that in
fact his older brothers have worked as hard for him as they
have for themselves. He gives an example, one of hundreds he could have cited. "Some years ago my older
brothers came to watch me record a song for release. It was
just before my voice changed. Actually it was the last song
I sang before going into the more adult style — in other
words, it was sung in my 'li'l boy voice.' They didn't come
to 'show me how,' they weren't there to pull my belt tighter
in case my 'li'l boy voice' slipped out of the groove and
dropped a couple of octaves. And they weren't there to
heckle or cajole. They were there because they were
genuinely concerned about me and about how the session
would go.

"It's been a good feeling to know that any time I
needed help, there was a wealth of it to call upon. It's
always been that way in our family. Sometimes people
write asking about my relationship with my family — they

seem to find it hard to comprehend a family where the members are not envious or jealous of each other. Yet what can I say? That's just how it is. Sure, we've had some disagreements, some minor irritations here and there. But it's over almost immediately. There's never been anything serious, never anything that lasts."

When you talk to Donny Osmond you know that he loves his large family. It was that atmosphere that made "growing up" fairly easy. In the family he was treated with the respect due him and his opinion was listened to, the same as with the six boys before him and the girl and boy who came after him.

Does he enjoy performing, or are there times when he'd just as soon be in some other occupation? "Well, on stage there's usually a high energy output, even though you may be trying to look relaxed. So there are bound to be times when you don't feel at your peak, and at those times you just go on and work harder at it to make it enjoyable. I certainly enjoy this work. If I didn't, I wouldn't be in it. I didn't *have* to be a member of the group, I *wanted* to be. My brothers didn't say 'Donny, get in.' I showed an interest in it and I worked hard at it; then I joined the group and became a full-fledged member when I was seven."

This seventh son enjoys various moods of music: classical, rhythm and blues, rock. He plays several instruments well — saxophone, harpsichord, trombone, clarinet, organ, banjo, bass, guitar — and is an exceptional pianist. But he does not consider his talents exceptional. He believes that most people are born with basic talents similar to those he and his brothers possess. "It's all a matter of perfecting what we've been given." His brothers agree. There are latent talents in everyone, they feel, which will respond to the spark of creativity, the resolution to

With piano
and mike

With admirers screaming and reaching

bring them out, the persistent effort to achieve or even to excel. It may be difficult for those of us whose voice at this point resembles the mating call of the Brooklyn Bridge to agree, especially when we hear the mellifluous tones of these young men. But music has more than one vehicle of expression. Perhaps these brothers are right, and musical and other talents are latent in each of us awaiting discovery and development.

For all his wide-eyed good looks, Donny's family claim that he's not as "sweet and innocent" as he looks. They say he's a practical joker, no less. Among his exploits they recall the time he put shaving cream all over their manager's hotel telephone — then phoned him at 2:00 a.m.; the day he short-sheeted another manager's bed; plastic insects in ice cubes floating in a friend's orange juice; Donny's disguised voice phoning home and offering a special deal on a set of kitchen appliances; the "black eye" he scared the family with just before they were due to perform, which he removed with soap and water two minutes before the show began.

Sometimes people need protection against a practical joker, but that's not the reason why Donny and his brothers are usually kept securely away from their fans. This is necessary to protect the fans and the Osmonds, as anyone will know who has witnessed or been involved in the hysteria of a crowd of ten thousand massed fans — anyone's fans!

The fan-performer syndrome has been hashed over by countless commentators, professional and otherwise. Psychologists: "It's a manifestation of the unrequited love of that particular age group." Psychiatrists: "Somehow and somewhere and at sometime, something was lacking in somebody." Entrepreneurs: "Aren't they wonderful?" Classical musicians: "Obviously something's haywire in

In Marie's
dressing room

On a Perry Como show

the auditory canal." Officer Gill Clancy of the mounted patrol: "It's the only time I've seen my horse go into shock." A mother: "Listen, she doesn't have enough strength to pick up her own sweater from her bedroom floor. How could she possibly have bent that door?" But regardless of the comments, the fan-performer association is a necessary one. The Osmonds genuinely appreciate it, and they go out of their way to help the fans through such media as their fan magazine.

Once when the brothers were sequestered on the top floor of a hotel, their fans below began to mill about and call for remembrances. "Throw us a souvenir," they shouted. The Osmonds comply with the fans' wishes whenever possible, but in this case, how? They'd had pizza that day, and the only thing that belonged to them in their room was the pizza and some balloons that Jay had bought. So like an edible flying saucer, the pizza took flight from the balcony.

"Throw us some more, throw us some more," came the cry.

"That's all there is."

"Well, throw us something."

About that time, Donny spotted the balloons. Filling several with water, he went to the balcony, hollered "Hi!" to his fans, and lofted the globular missiles. The crowd surged to catch the objects; then, suddenly realizing what was descending, they tried to retrace their steps. Too late! Several were christened when the balloons struck heads, shoulders and pavement. Perhaps the saturated felt as though something very personal had taken place between themselves and Donny, and they raised their arms over their heads and chanted, "Thank you! Thank you!'"

Donny certainly looks a picture of health, but he has not had a problemless life in this respect. A pain started when he was nine years old, a light nagging in the stomach area. Occasionally it would reach an intensity which compelled him to double over. After a while it would abate. He could not eat certain foods without discomfort. The doctors became concerned because he had a difficult time gaining weight. Extensive examination showed nothing. Nerves, emotions, personality and diet were considered, but no conclusion was forthcoming. Barium tests, x-rays, and blood tests all produced negative results.

The doctors had answers, but not the crucial one. Yes, he probably had the pain. No, the doctors didn't think he was a malingerer. Yes, there is such a thing as psychosomatically induced pain. No, they didn't think he was capable of inducing pain himself. So it went on. They just didn't know.

The pains persisted through the tenth year, the eleventh, the twelfth; and finally, around his thirteenth birthday, they stopped. He remained free from the distress for almost a calendar year. The doctors assumed that whatever the problem had been, it had worked itself out.

But like the volcano which goes to sleep for a season and then returns with a horrendous howl of awakening, Donny's pain returned. Now it lasted for a longer time and with an intensity so acute as to make Donny immobile. Then it began to double him up. There were more tests, with the same results as before. Finally, on a day when he could no longer bear the pain, when it twisted his face and made tears run uncontrolled down his cheeks, the doctors decided they must "open him up." At that time Donny Osmond went down in history as having one of the longest and largest appendixes ever removed.

Medically interesting as this fact was, something
else interested the doctors more. The sac-like appendage
was replete with scar tissue — not just a few, but scores of
lesions running the length of the appendix. It baffled
them. How could that appendix have nearly ruptured and
then healed itself so many times? Here was another medical question which could not be explained in medical
terms.

But Donny knew the answer. So did his brothers
and his parents. While they hadn't known what Donny's
ailment was, from the condition of the appendix as de-
scribed they knew exactly what had happened.

Donny reads from the scriptures every day, and like
his family he feels he has good cause to believe implicitly
in the words of James in the Bible: "Is any sick among you?
Let him call for the elders of the church; and let them pray
over him. . . . And the prayer of faith shall save the sick,
and the Lord shall raise him up. . . ." Donny's father and
older brothers are elders of his Church. In his pain he had
"called for" them. They had laid their hands on his head
and "prayed over him." This "prayer of faith" had stopped
the attacks before they became full-blown ruptures, and
the scar tissues now evidenced the repeated healing pro-
cesses. "I didn't know what was going on inside me," says
Donny, "but I know that when my father and brothers laid
their hands on my head and blessed me, the pain left me —
usually, right away."

A simple faith? Perhaps. The Osmonds are simple
people — in the best sense of that term.

12   *The Show Goes On*

A young man, temporarily out of control, left his seat at one of the performances and ran up to the stage. He stood there with his shirt open. Stuck in his belt was a gun. His eyes were glazed, his body trembling, his breathing rapid. He fixed his stare on Merrill, who was in the middle of a popular song with the group.

What does a performer do under such circumstances? No primer for entertainers would supply the answer. What Merrill did was to return the troubled youngster's look and to project both personality and voice at him as the song continued. A line in the song goes, "I can tell you've been hurt by the look on your face." At this phrasing the young man stopped trembling and slowly made his way back from the stage.

A close call? Who knows? It's very difficult sometimes to measure the difference between potential danger and immediate danger. The brothers found themselves wondering what the young man's problem was.

Young men in the audience at a show in France clearly had a different problem. Theirs was that they wanted to make trouble, perhaps because they resented the attention the predominantly girl audience was giving the Osmonds.

The show was going well when the doors burst open and in surged a French version of Hell's Angels, leather jackets and all. Soon the place was in an uproar as these hoodlums pelted the performers with potatoes and other projectiles. "They hurt, too," Wayne remembers. "And one of these fellows hit Father in the head with an egg." The attempt to break up the show foundered at the end of some well-placed fists when the group's security guards were able to come to grips with the problem, and the disturbers were hustled out, looking if possible even less angelic than when they arrived.

That problem at least was visible, but how about being the center of a bomb scare? It happened at Madison Square Garden in New York. Olive remembers it well.

"Marie and I were downstairs in the dressingroom. Some of the fans had brought gifts for the boys, as often happens, and we were going to get the address details so that we could send thank-you notes. We decided to open the packages so that we could repack them for carrying them on the bus. Suddenly four policemen were dashing towards us shouting, 'Don't touch those boxes!' They alone scared the wits out of us, quite apart from the news of a phone call saying that a bomb might go off at any time."

"They went through everything," Merrill remembers, "the garbage cans, the gifts, our equipment, underneath the stage. It held up the show for a while. Fortunately they didn't find any bomb."

There was no bomb in Memphis, Tennessee, but there was a lot of damage. The security arrangements at the hotel were poor, and when the Osmonds checked in, the fans were already there and swarming over the building. Within minutes they had located the Osmond suite and were running unchecked up and down the hallways and in front of the Osmonds' rooms. Since the best chance for safety lay in consolidating their forces and their belongings, the family carried all their trunks and cases and costumes into the room shared by Wayne and Alan, piled them there, then locked the door. The family then all assembled in the room next door, the main room of the suite. There they had a meal brought up and sat around relaxing and watching TV.

After about half an hour of this, Marie thought she heard a movement in the next room. "I think there's someone next door," she said. They all listened, but decided she was mistaken. Five minutes later Marie again thought she picked up an unusual noise. They checked, but everyone was accounted for and the door to the next room was still locked. Soon after that the power went off. Now there came cries of "Fire! Fire!" and when they stepped out into the hallway there was smoke pouring from underneath the door of Alan and Wayne's room.

Quickly they unlocked the door, and thick black smoke billowed out at them. There was nothing to do but get out, which by now was the urgent aim of the occupants of that floor. Everyone made for the fire escape door. It was locked — presumably as a means of keeping fans out. Luckily the lead trumpet player of the Osmonds' rhythm section was a black belt in karate, and with a hefty side-kick he broke open the door. Everyone got out without injury.

The contents of the smoke-filled room were not so fortunate. They were totally demolished. By the time the fire department had extinguished the fire, soaking everything to insure that nothing could smolder into flame, the roomful of props and personal belongings had degenerated into a mess of charred, sodden, and frequently unrecognizable objects which someone had shoveled into a big pile.

Fortunately the boys' instruments were safe. In the bus too was a set of costumes — dirty, waiting to be cleaned, but available in this emergency. The brothers gave their usual high-spirited, high-quality performance in their show that night as if nothing untoward had happened that day.

An entertainer needs to have a positive attitude like that, for as with many other occupations there is a drudgery connected with show business. It is that day-to-day "getting up" for each performance and knowing that, regardless of how low you feel, you must do your best. With some performers the axiom is old hat, and they will cancel a performance for anything from a hangnail to a hangover, but with the Osmonds the old slogan is still valid — "The show must go on." So far as they are concerned, each audience is new. "They have paid their money to see a show, and we try to give them the very best show that's in us." They work hard to this end.

In keeping with this spirit, the group has performed with sprained joints, broken bones, lacerated feet and hands, and various degrees of colds, flu, and other common ailments. "There's no way in the world that I could ever sit back and watch the other guys working on the stage without me. I'd go out if I had to crawl." Alan's sentiments find reverification in the other brothers.

A vivid example of this took place in Indianapolis, when the brothers were playing two shows a day to speedway crowds. They had a karate routine in their act in which Alan and Jay would take turns sparring. The action was tight and close in. Jay tells it best — as indeed he should! "There was one move where Alan kneed me in the

Harmony and timing – significant to a karate act as to a singing routine

stomach, and this time he accidentally kneed me too hard and knocked all the wind out of me. So instead of going back, I doubled up and my head went forward. This wasn't in the act, so Alan wasn't ready for it, and he came back with his usual swing — a roundhouse which smacked my nose and broke it in four places."

"It all happened so fast that at first I didn't realize I'd hit him," recalls Alan. "But there was blood streaming from his nose. We just all stopped, and here we were with ten to fifteen thousand people in the grandstands and us just in the middle of the show."

The impulse was, "we have to finish the show." The audience had paid their good money and they deserved the best from the brothers. What to do? Even for the resourceful Osmonds, this was a tough one.

"I went to the microphone," says Alan, "and said 'We'll have to take a break here for a second. I accidentally hit my brother and gave him a bloody nose (I didn't want to say it was broken, because that sounded awful) so we're going to go down and have a word of prayer. We'll be back in five minutes.' When I finished I couldn't believe I'd said that."

At this point Olive and Marie were under the bleachers in the ticket office. A man walked by and they heard him say, "Boy, it's sure too bad what happened to Jay Osmond." "We dropped what we were doing and took off," says Marie, "and as we were running across the speedway to get to where the boys were, the audience all started clapping. As we ran down the steps, there was a whole trail of blood."

Olive recalls: "We got down there just in time to join the prayer circle. It was that bad, and we felt we needed guidance on whether they should go on with the show or not. As the prayer ended, Jay said, 'Well, I don't know about the rest of you, but if the show's going to go on, you'd better follow me quick.' He was the first one to leave.''

The show was resumed, with the Osmonds' manager standing behind Jay pinching his nose together with a towel while Jay sang and did his drum solos. He played the drums as hard as ever. The nose almost stopped bleeding until they had finished that show, but as soon as they got off stage the blood started running again. With another show still to do that day, there was no time now to get the nose set, but at least it could be sewn up. That day was the only day during the fair that a plastic surgeon had checked into the fair grounds to offer his services for emergencies. He sewed up Jay's nose, and for good measure he put a few stitches in Alan's offending knuckle, which had got itself cut open on Jay's bone.

The entertainer's life is never easy, but neither is it normally as hard as that engagement some years back at a fair in New Jersey. The Osmonds were the headliners and occupied nearly half of the show. There were five or six other acts, each of which naturally did a much smaller stint, perhaps ten minutes each. All this sounds fine — except that the contract required the performers to do a show whenever there was an audience.

The trouble was, there was always an audience. The performers were doing as many as six shows a day, even though most of the acts involved a lot of physical activity. "The place would fill up, the other acts would go out and kind of give us a chance to breathe, then we'd go out and do our show. But there was no closing time. The management would let the place clear out then fill up again; then the first act would start right up and we were on the way again. This went on and on for a couple of weeks, and it got

Donny's hat sails out into the crowd

The umpteenth airport wait

to a point towards the end that the first acts couldn't take it, and they would have to do alternate shows. But we had to do every show, and what with singing, tap dancing, and playing saxophones we were just beat. That was one of the hardest shows we ever did."

One of the brothers looks further back, to the years when they used to tour fairs with Andy Williams. "Not only would we do our own show on stage and then work with Andy on stage, but we also had to be in the wings singing background parts into a mike. We sang for most of the show. It was really rough."

There have been times when the brothers have done six performances a day over a lengthy period, and this can have a devastating effect on the vocal chords. This kind of schedule, or sore throat, colds, or laryngitis, or a combination of such circumstances, has caught up with each one of them many times, making one or the other hoarse at performance time, perhaps unable to sing at all. In this situation the remainder of the group will sing a little louder while the afflicted one does what he can — even if he just moves his mouth to "lip-sync" the song.

The brothers know each others' parts so well that each one can readily switch. Frequently Alan will sense a loss of voice in one of the performers; and because of the closeness of the group and their long association, by a signal which the audience cannot detect he will be able to shift the parts. Merrill does a lot of solo work, for instance, and on some days his voice will become tired. Alan knows Merrill has to be strong at the end, so at Alan's signal he will take the solo and Merrill will revamp in the mike position and save his voice. Alternatively Merrill will solo for Alan, Jay will take Merrill's part, and Alan will take Jay's. "All Alan has to do is to give us a look and we know what to do," says Merrill.

With their brand of resourcefulness, the brothers have restaged numbers with incredible speed, finesse and quality. Wayne will break a guitar string, and Alan will take his part. Jay has broken four drums on different occasions, and when that happens the boys will tap on the hand mikes to simulate the sound of drums. "We cover for each other all the time," says Wayne. "The audience has come to enjoy themselves, and normally they're not supposed to know if something goes wrong. But with so many people and instruments and movements on stage, something can easily go wrong. Our job is to make it sound and look right."

By the time they have a number ready it certainly sounds right. It has taken them all of their fifteen or sixteen years to achieve the blend of close harmony for which they are noted, but they don't rest on any laurels when it comes to arranging and rehearsing. As to their show looking right, while it does that too there is nothing artificial about it. The brothers are not easily put out, but what does "bug" them is the suggestion sometimes made that they are not really playing all those instruments.

Naturally they have the same criterion for recordings as well — make it right, make it good. They have spent countless hours of practice for every hour of performance, and their proficiency is such that time after time they have come to the recording or television studies so well prepared that over the years they have become known as the one-take Osmonds. "It's rewarding to look back at a song we've done, say, two or three years ago and know that it still sounds good, the message is still clear. 'Hey! that's me singing,' I say, 'and it's not too bad.' We take a lot of pride in what we do, and its good to know it has a lasting quality." Jay's reflection is echoed by the others.

This means working as hard to stay at the top as they

did to get there. No let-down, no assumption that their popularity or prestige will make up for sloppy performance or mediocre songs. "The kids are getting a lot smarter these days. They're really listening to the records — more than they used to. The Beatles made a mistake on this one. Paul McCartney once said that the Beatles were so popular that even if they recorded 'Mary Had a Little Lamb' they would have a hit record. Well, they recorded it; and it was the biggest bomb they have ever had. It showed that people would not go out and buy a Beatle record any more just because it was a Beatle record. These days you have to prove yourself and keep proving yourself."

Selection criteria for their songs are a mixture of instinct and experience. The audience response to an on-stage number is frequently predictable as to both timing and duration and is a fairly safe guide to the recording side of the business too. They perform both the songs of others, adapted as necessary, and those they write themselves. When a song they receive is weak, sometimes they can tighten the lyrics or the music, as required, put a good soundtrack behind it, and make a successful recording out of it. What they look for is a catchy song, one that keeps going through the listener's head when the record is over. However good it may be otherwise, its success is in doubt without this quality.

Most of the Osmonds' songwriting is done by Alan, Wayne and Merrill. It's a convenient situation in several ways. The brothers are devoid of the temperamental problems that afflict many entertainers, and their easy relationship permits a very frank interchange. "We frequently work on a very high energy level," explains Merrill, "so this frankness is very important. Perhaps Al will write a song and I'll tell him it's one of the worst songs I ever heard. But he knows I'm criticizing the song; he doesn't

Many thousands attend outdoor concerts . . .

and some have to be restrained

take it as a criticism of himself, and there are no hurt feelings. And it's the same whichever one of us has done the writing."

With this kind of mutual attitude and their high criteria for songwriting, they approach the task in many different ways, from Alan's sitting down and "I've just got to write a song," to Merrill's inspiration in the shower, to Donny's and Jay's rapid exit from the dinner table to pick out notes on the piano. Some they struggle with, while some seem to appear magically as if from space. As to lyrics, the brothers feel that a song should make a statement, but since even good statements will fail if linked to mediocre music, there has to be a fine wedding of lyrics and music. When the listener subconsciously says, "I can relate to that" and a majority of listeners feel that way, chances are the songwriter has a hit on his hands.

Once the song is arranged and rehearsed, it's a matter of getting it "laid down" — recorded, that is. They don't have to go halfway across the nation to do this any more — it's done in their own recording studio at home. "Being able to do this at home helps a lot," says Wayne. "So does having skilled people like an Ed Green and a Mike Curb, who have been working with us since we started recording, and who know our sounds, and so on. They know what types of microphones to use for a certain sound, for backgrounds, for lead vocals. When we record, the rest of us will go into the other room and work on the background part while one guy is recording his lead. When he gets finished, the background part will move into the studio and we will put that on the recording. It's a continuous thing; sometimes we work right around the clock. All this makes recording much quicker and more efficient."

Whether using their own or others' songs, the Osmonds keep changing and experimenting. Marie sings country and western, Donny sings the love ballads, Jimmy has snappy, catchy tunes. The group is highly contemporary, which means that they must keep changing because their listeners are changing.

With one exception, one change they don't have to be concerned about any more is changing voices. A boy's change of voice is normally no big deal, but for a singing group it makes a lot of difference. Whereas Alan had the baritone part first, with the maturing of Wayne's voice he went back to low tenor. Merrill was then singing the high parts and Jay the melody. When Merrill's voice changed and he went to tenor, Donny filled the upper range he vacated. Donny's "Oh, give it one more chance before you give up on love" in that boyish soprano has thrilled thousands throughout the world. That voice in its turn has now been stilled and the "high calling" has fallen to Jimmy. With voice changes of course there came much rearranging of songs and learning of new parts. This meant discarding stacks of music, arrangements that had cost thousands of dollars.

As a young act, there were other changes they couldn't control, and although there was a certain hand-me-down dimension when their costumes were all look-alike, it was still difficult to get any longevity out of the apparel. This was a matter for careful economic management, for in the early days every penny that came in was put on the boys' backs, in their mouths, or onto music lessons and instruments. To conserve funds, the family would meticulously watch extra baggage weight when using airlines. The boys remember washing out socks and underwear at night and hanging them in the bathroom. In an extremity on one occasion, Jay slept in the bathtub.

When it became possible for Olive to travel with

them, only slightly larger accommodation was permissible. They would eat in their hotel or motel room, which usually contained two beds and four rollaways. George and Olive would leave the motel room with their suitcases, an act liable to be looked upon with suspicion unless their rent had been paid in advance. They would go to the local grocer and bring back in the suitcases such fare as juices, fresh fruit, bread, bologna, mayonnaise, and other foods requiring no cooking. The boys recall having eaten an ocean-full of oysters in such circumstances, which perhaps accounts for their profound dislike for that bottom-dwelling marine mollusk. The proprietors of many a motel-restaurant must have been somewhat curious about a well-fed, healthy looking family which never seemed to patronize the restaurant.

In the early days it was hard to get past those lower rungs of the ladder, and there was more than one false step. Having gone to Pasadena, California, to do a show, the group had once again tried to reach Lawrence Welk without success, so the trip back was already edged with some feeling of disappointment. In Las Vegas they went to the TV station, and there Martin Black had the boys sing on his show. It was there that a performer saw the boys and, so to speak, fell for them. At her invitation they went to see her show at the Desert Inn that night.

Heading the billing was a top-line singing star, and after the show she took the boys to his dressingroom. "I think he can do something for you," she told them. "These kids are talented; they just need someone to give them the right break." Olive remembers it this way:

"He listened to the boys, and the tears ran down his cheeks as they sang 'I wouldn't trade the silver in my mother's hair for all the gold in the world.' He said, 'I'm going to be doing a show in May. For Mother's Day, will you bring your boys back and let them sing this song with me on the stage in Vegas?' Of course, we thought maybe that was our lucky break. We came home and the boys rehearsed and rehearsed; they really had that song polished. But we didn't hear any more about the Vegas engagement. It was one more disappointment."

For eight years before they headlined at Caesar's Palace in Las Vegas they worked as second and third bananas, and during that time they ran into some pretty skimpy situations on stage as well as off. They have dressed behind hanging blankets and in kitchens, performed when rain and a thunderstorm reduced the music to a cacophony. They have performed in a rodeo arena after it had been abused by the cowboys, horses, bulls, and rain; and on one such occasion they had to walk through knee-deep mud to get to the stage.

If the facilities have frequently been less than ideal, the Osmonds learned over the years that they could never be sure what kind of local talent the agent would arrange for as the band. They have had musicians wander in short minutes before the performance and not be ready for curtain time. They have had them come in drunk and absolutely worthless as band members. They have had them show up in the middle of a performance — or not show up at all. They have had bands backing their instrumentals which were so bad that they have had the band sit there mute while they performed without them. They have had bands that lost the rhythm, and Alan has conducted them while the group sang. They have had big promoters say, "Sure! You bet! Yes, we'll get you that! It's a big, well-known orchestra!" — then on their arrival the "big band" has materialized in the shape of a five-piece rock group whose only criterion seemed to be "the louder, the better."

To provide last-minute music when let down, they

This act ("Rockin' & Rollin' 50's") always delights the audience

With the septet all together, so does this one

have purchased tape recorders, wired them into the P.A. system, and used a demo tape of the music. "I think we belong to every union in the book," muses Merrill. "We like to jump in and get things moving, and we've had our hands slapped on several occasions." Small wonder that now they take their own nine-piece band with them when they perform, and that they always get there early to check instruments, equipment, and stage facilities.

In setting things up for their act they have developed a knack for working with people. While they will not compromise ideals, they are flexible where ideas are concerned. They get the stage hands on their side by open friendliness. They have learned to be diplomatic with technicians and camera crews. They know that in theory none of this should be necessary, but in any case it's much more natural for them to lay out the honey than the vinegar, and with this approach they can generally motivate others to do what is needed and do it willingly.

How have the Osmonds been received outside of their native land? While fans put out the welcome mat for them now in both Europe and the Orient, it took time and effort to get to this point. "We didn't just walk into other countries as a known group," Merrill remembers. "We had to go there and work hard to establish ourselves. I remember that we walked down Carnaby Street in London and nobody knew us. We were just like tourists to them. If we'd lined up, we couldn't have given our autographs away. Then right after that Donny's record 'Puppy Love' hit. Our records hit. Then we couldn't be seen anywhere in England. Since then, in England Donny has been voted the number one male vocalist for albums, and Jimmy the number one male vocalist for singles."

It was the same in any country — "We had to put our licks in and start at the bottom and work up." Recalling their first tour in Japan brings smiles to the boys' faces. Once people came to their show they'd be captured, but how were they to get them there the first time? The Japanese agent had the answer.

"There was a little bus or van they'd pick us up in at the airport, and there were loudspeakers on top of it. The driver would be talking through these speakers in Japanese as we went along. It seemed to be a long way to the hotel until we realized what was going on — we were 'on display,' so to speak, and passers-by were being invited to our show. It was rather like being part of a traveling zoo, but that's how we got people to come to our first concert in Japan."

The language barrier was more of a problem then than it is now, the Osmonds feel, but in any case it has been their practice to learn one song in the native tongue of the country they were visiting. Young Jimmy's "Red Roses for a Blue Lady" he learned in Japanese before leaving America, but for their joint effort the group had someone in Japan choose a popular song and sing it into a tape recorder in Japanese. They then sat around the tape recorder and played the song back over and over again until they had learned it phonetically. Singing it on stage seemed to establish a rapport with the people.

What really got them going in Japan was the television medium, Olive feels. "One of our friends in Japan got the kids some exposure on several different TV shows. Then Jimmy happened to break his arm and got newspaper headlines, and he went directly to the TV station to perform with the arm in a cast. Everywhere we went people would pat him on the head and be sympathetic. It was just wonderful how kind and loving the Japanese people were to him."

George sees such things in very practical terms. "I

In rehearsal

In the mirror, just before a performance

believe our success is due a lot to a series of gimmicks. It started with Jay following the TV cameras on the Andy Williams show. Then along came Donny, and he was a gimmick all the way. Then came Jimmy with a broken arm that turned people's hearts to him. Now came Marie and Donny together, and this is hitting too. I don't care how good you are, you've got to have a gimmick to be a success in this business."

In Sweden too on one of their tours there were some unusual attempts to arrest the public attention. A new zoo was opening at the time, and since the Osmonds were getting a lot of press publicity they were persuaded to link that publicity with the zoo's to the expected benefit of both. Accordingly the boys were photographed in various zoo-like poses — feeding the elephant, in front of the lions' cage, holding monkeys. Then the photographer had a bright idea. Over there was a couple of camels. Just the thing — a picture of the Osmonds on a camel!

There's not much room for two people between the humps of a camel, as Merrill and Jay soon discovered, but their distaste of the position was as nothing compared to the camel's. Meanwhile Alan and Wayne had been persuaded to mount the other camel, which was even bigger, blacker, shaggier, and of meaner disposition than Merrill and Jay's unwilling steed. But any fears were unfounded, they were assured. In fact, the zoo attendant told them, it would make a better shot if they would just let go of the rein. The camels wouldn't run away, he promised.

Alan and Wayne in particular found themselves hoping that their camel was equally confident on this point, and that the gruntings and squirmings of this "ship of the desert" beneath them didn't mean that it was getting up steam. In this case their fears would have been a surer guide than their hopes, for while they tried to hide both their apprehensions and their discomfort under a some-what forced photogenic smile the camel decided it had had enough of all this malarkey and took off for the seclusion of its shed.

The fit between those humps had been tight enough before, but like a bag of wheat the two boys were now shaken down more surely into position with every painful step of this loping quadruped. Pinched and hurting, the boys simply couldn't get off. With Alan wedged behind him, Wayne couldn't get his leg up and over the front hump; and Alan was in the same desperate straits behind with respect to the rear protuberance. What to do? Chance and the incessant jolting solved the problem for Wayne, who tumbled off sideways, landing under the camel and narrowly escaping its flailing hooves. Only slightly less uncomfortable now and not one whit less scared, Alan held on, ducking his head smartly to avoid decapitation as the long-legged beast sailed through the doorway of its shed. Honor was satisfied when the black-hearted creature had run Alan's leg into a metal beam, and it then came to rest. With an ankle the size of a grapefruit, Alan would dance in the show that evening.

That slow, steady progress up the ladder of success which the brothers have made through the years has brought one interesting kind of difficulty the family could never have envisaged. As their fame has grown, so have the on-tour restrictions — being confined to a hotel floor, even locked in a hotel room on occasions. Donny in particular can find it difficult to get a little fresh air and exercise when the brothers are staying in a place replete with alert, eager teeny-boppers. He has been known to overcome this problem by going for a walk with George or one of the brothers at three or four in the morning. So there's a price to pay for everything, even fame.

For all the fame, the brothers don't forget those early, lean years or the two people who through those years guided them to success. Now as then, one of their strongest motivating forces is their sincere desire to please their parents. In the days when money and opportunity were scarce, now and again the boys would optimistically look ahead with a pledge. "Just think, Father, when we make it big we can buy you a little motel just like that one over there." They would lean toward that side of the car to measure the magnanimity of the projected gift. Alternatively it would be, "How do you like that ranch over there, Father? Well, maybe we can buy you one just like that someday." Parents and offspring alike now enjoy the benefits as they reflect on the correctness of that early decision to invest in those natural talents.

Many hundreds of performances after that decision, the show still goes on.

13 *Marie*

Waiting in the wings, Marie Osmond nervously smoothed the pleats of her full-length blue chiffon dress. There must be easier places than Caesar's Palace in Las Vegas to make your solo debut on the American stage, especially when you weren't yet quite fourteen years old, but here she was anyway. And after all, she had had a taste of cabaret performing the previous spring in that duet she had done with Donny.

On stage the brothers had finished a number and were taking a bow. Marie didn't know whether to be glad or sorry for the lengthy applause. Was she frightened! We . . e . . ll, not exactly. But nervous. Under her mother's watchful eye she'd checked her hair, her dream dress. She knew the song — it was her newest release. Everything would be okay.

The applause tailed off, and she could hear Alan introducing her. The brothers parted and gave her the stage as she walked on, her face alight with the Osmond smile. This was it. She was on!

She recalls that the walking on was the worst part, and that soon her nerves calmed down. Even so, it would be much easier after the first night. The audience thought she was terrific with her rendition of "Paper Roses." To

Olive Marie Osmond

Marie, her two weeks of rehearsals for that act paid off. She felt good about her performance. But the Osmonds have no experience in the swelled-head department, and the old-trouper brothers set the record straight. "Oh, that was a good show tonight. But you'll do better on the second show." And they were right.

They perhaps aren't always right, but they sure have the voting power. How does it feel to be the only girl in a prominent family where she is outnumbered eight to one? How does it feel to be one of the most envied girls in the world, not alone for her own talents, which are impressive, but because of her close proximity to the Osmond brothers? Now that she is recognized worldwide as having fine talent in her own right, has she experienced any attitude changes? How does she respond to such questions?

"Well, as for me being the only girl, that's kind of an interesting situation. I've had a lot of girls come up to me and ask, 'How do you get along with your brothers?' Well, we get along with each other fine. Most of the time I let the boys have their way. And when my friends say, 'Don't you ever fight back?' — well, I think it's stupid to fight, especially with eight of them, all except one older than me. How could I win? So if there was something I felt strongly enough about and they disagreed, I'd find a gentler way to go about it. And anyway, why would I want to quarrel with my family?"

Marie gets along well with her family because she respects them all. Of her parents she says: "They are such great teachers. I remember once I was upset because Mother made me wear a dress I didn't want to wear. I thought it made me look fat. I kind of got upset at her, and I shouldn't have done that. I remember Father taking me aside and saying, 'You never, never, *ever* yell at your

Earlier days —
a young traveler

mother, *ever!*' It really impressed me. He said, 'Your mother loves you more than anyone else does in this world, just as I love you more than anyone else does in this world; and the only reason she would want you to wear that dress is that she thinks it's best for you.' I remember that as if it were yesterday. My father taught me to have respect not only for Mother and himself but for my brothers. After all, I've come along near the end, and my brothers have helped me to learn how to get along with myself and others, as well as how to be a performing Osmond."

The Osmonds' fan magazine naturally attracts a lot of letters — several thousand a week. A great many are directed to Marie. Frequently the writer sees in Marie one she can relate to as a girl of her own age and who obviously belongs to a highly united and successful family. Some of the "secrets" of that unity and success stand out to fans who have not had the same experiences. Of all things, they often mention discipline — with approval!

"I receive letters from girls who feel that maybe their fathers don't love them because they don't discipline them. 'It must be neat to have someone discipline you,' they say. It seems that a lot of kids want their parents to love them but the parents don't know how to show that love. They think they're showing their love by giving the kids everything they want.

"I've never got all I wanted, just for the asking — none of us have. When we wanted something, we would discuss it with our parents and they would say, 'Yes, you can have it,' or 'No, I don't think you should have it.' And that was that. And I certainly never felt unloved if they refused. Of course, any time I got a spanking I didn't feel very good about it at the time, but that feeling soon wore off, whereas the feeling of being loved was always there. I

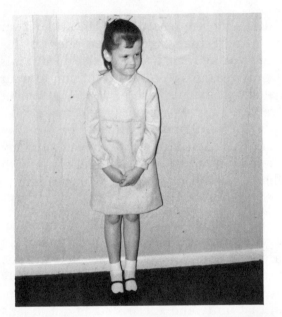

Growing up . . .

. . . to be a beautiful
young lady

see now that taking the trouble to discipline me was one way my parents showed their love for me. I'm very glad they did it."

Discussion of discipline invariably brings Marie to that bane of the teen-ager's existence — chores. How does she make out in this area? Maybe she's just temperamentally suited to housework or something, but she'll actually tell you she doesn't mind doing it at all. "When you're in a large family you learn to help each other and to do your chores, and mine is to try to keep the house in order. I keep the kitchen clean and the living room and the dining room. Sometimes I don't do too good a job, but, you know — well, it's kind of a big job. I believe it helps me get ready to take care of my own home when I get married, so I guess that's another advantage of belonging to a big family."

Marriage. You're thinking of marriage, Marie? What about your career as a singer? Marie has firm and clear views on such matters. "My ultimate goal is to be a wife and mother. That's more important to me in the long run than show business, though of course I enjoy singing and hope there are good years ahead for me in that career."

But won't that maybe frustrate her somewhat, to be "put down a notch," as some have expressed it to her? "People who ask that kind of question simply don't understand. Just because you're not in the public eye, that doesn't mean you're somehow living an inferior life. I don't think there's any greater role than the parent's. And the man's is not greater than the woman's — it's just different. He's the provider and the head of the family. The woman is his equal partner. She's the mother, and she raises the children and tries to set them a good example. What's more important than that role? It's been that way in our family, and I want the same kind of setup when I have a home of my own."

Where does that leave women's lib? "Some of what they're trying to do is okay, I guess. If a girl is a good mechanic, she shouldn't be kept from working in an auto shop just because she's a girl, for instance. Equal pay for equal work is another thing that makes sense. But personally I can't agree with a lot of the women's lib philosophies, like when they get men's and women's roles mixed, as it seems to me."

Marie knows there are many who think otherwise — and that's their privilege, she feels. Others may feel to question her "authority," so to speak. What can a girl so young know of such matters? Who is this young lady who speaks with such assurance and conviction?

It's true, as her friends and family recall, that a few short years ago Marie was just a child, with no particular interest in the family career, no concept of her own potential as an entertainer, and certainly no aspirations to "set the world to rights" — even the world of the girls who now write by the thousand seeking her counsel. In those days she was too busy enjoying the long summer days of play and the Bible bedtime stories from Mother that followed them, rolling with Donny in the Utah snow, or savoring the fantasies the mind would readily create in the childhood dreamhouse in Canoga Park. The older boys remember her as a tomboy when she was seven or eight. How could she be otherwise, with so many older brothers she just had to join with and imitate as they played baseball, climbed a tree, did some tricky acrobatics, or indulged in the myriad other activities of energetic youth?

The pattern didn't change too much over the next few years. Marie was especially close to Donny, confident with him, and something of a "big sister" figure with Jimmy. "At twelve," the boys recall, "she was a nice kid — wise for her age, but still a kid — with a hint of a babyface

Famous sister with famous brother

Moods of Marie

still, no makeup, tousled hair, and jeans and a shirt." The change came quickly, as it does to girls around that age. Gigi-like, suddenly at thirteen she went through the metamorphosis and emerged as the poised and beautiful girl she now is, with a good singing voice and a number one record all over the world. She still likes to wear jeans, but the rest of the childhood world is now well behind her.

Like Donny and, later, Jimmy, Marie was under no compulsion to "join the club" of the performing Osmonds. She did it because she wanted to and because both she and they could tell that that ol' Osmond talent was there. She made her true stage debut in Sweden when not quite seven years old. The brothers were on tour — *really* on tour, Marie recollects, since they were doing three shows a day in three different towns, and seemed to do nothing else but perform, travel, and change costumes. Her memory of those days is hazy, but she recalls wearing a red costume and being taught the Swedish words to her song by a local blond lady. Then she went out and wowed the audience with a country western tune that was sung all over Sweden — "If you loved me half as much as I love you."

Those Swedish words might fade, but the essence of the experience of that tour would forever be a part of her. Perhaps it was the beginning of the quiet confidence she was to feel later when she began singing in earnest. Given her abundant talent, apparently as a gift from the genes, acquiring "stage presence" was admittedly not as tough for her as it might have been for someone breaking in on her own. The brothers had been along the route. They showed her the ropes, taught her what to do and what not to do on stage to make things work for her. "My older brothers had it much tougher than I did," she acknowledges. "By the time I came along, those early years were over and the boys were well established. I was able to fit in." Her brothers' positive attitude toward the business helped. Nobody told her the footlights and the audience were things to fear, and that kind of attitude encouraged her to develop confidence.

A few years after her Swedish debut, Marie accompanied the family on the brothers' 1970 Japanese tour. In another exercise in linguistics she sang in the Japanese tongue, this time the then current favorite "Raindrops Keep Fallin' on My Head." It wasn't long after this that the family made a discovery — that was her kind of music.

When they had her singing and dancing to a song like "Peg o' My Heart," one of her earlier efforts, one of the boys would be gently prodding her in the back and saying "Sing up! Sing up!" But when she let loose on a song like "Raindrops" she overpowered the mike. Her mother claims credit for first spotting the country and western flavor of Marie's voice. That voice would go on to bigger and better things.

Marie makes her voice heard off the stage as well as on, in real life as well as in the glamor world of show business. She is no "dumb brunette." While she is modest in expression and in no way conceited, she is intelligent, has numerous hobbies, and is interested in what is happening in the world around her. Furthermore she has an unusual maturity of thought and character. Naturally she expresses opinions on some of the significant facets of life as she sees them.

"Girls write to me about moral standards, about physical relationships with boys. They ask what I think. Well, to my mind any immorality is wrong, and just as much wrong before marriage as after. It's wrong in God's eyes. But it's foolish too because it cheapens and weakens the relationship. And it's just as wrong for the boy as it is for the girl.

With Father

With Jay
and Merrill

With Bob Hope

With Donny
in TV special

"I know a girl who got involved in that kind of life before she got straightened out — there's no need to get married, you can just live together, and so on. I've talked to her about it. In that life, she said, she just wasn't happy; nothing really mattered; she wasn't getting anywhere; and she had no sense of a lasting relationship with a boy. 'Now,' she told me, 'I see why it's so important to be selective in choosing a mate. I was using the wrong basis for that choice.' "

If you press Marie, she'll enlarge on this a bit as regards her own expectations. "Somewhere out there is my Mr. Right. When we're both old enough I'll meet him, and we'll know we're for each other. Neither of us will have any past relationships to regret. We'll get married and raise a family. I'll be just for him, and he'll be just for me. We'll belong completely and forever."

Pending those larger successes, today's challenges await attention. Already Marie has had considerable success in the recording field and on the stage and has appeared on national television with such celebrities as Mike Douglas and Bob Hope. Undoubtedly there are higher levels of success ahead. Is the road a hard one for her? "People think I had an 'in' to the big-time because of my family, and of course there's a lot of truth in that. But I have to work for it too. In show business you don't achieve without a lot of effort."

On the matter of success, Marie is too modest to mention that she has been helped by a voice and a standard of performance that caused her to be voted the top country and western singer in America — an accolade she didn't get just by having famous brothers. She's modest in another area too — her dress. "I realize that if you've got Donny Osmond for a brother you won't be the most unpopular girl around. But really, you don't have to compromise on dress styles to be popular. My older brothers married some pretty nice girls, and they weren't attracted to them by immodest clothing — in fact, that would have turned them off."

Marie gets her mature thinking partly from family training and partly from reading and studying. The family influence has virtually eliminated the "generation gap" which plagues so many households. Marie can get eloquent about her parents. "I think all kids relate to someone or something, and I think if I had to pick an idol it would be my mother. She's a super-cool lady. She's really neat. I hope someday I can be just like her.

"Our parents have always been very understanding. A lot of parents will say rock music is for long-haired hippy freaks. Our parents actually listen to rock and try to relate to it, and we listen to their music. They give freely of themselves, which really helps out a lot, and I believe my brothers and I try to give of ourselves too and to see our parents' viewpoint. We don't agree on everything, but we do on most things, especially Mother and myself. When I changed so suddenly around fourteen or so, my tastes switched totally — it was a little hard for Mother to get used to. I grew up kind of fast, and my mother wasn't quite ready for it. But she adjusted quickly."

As for studying, the erratic schedule of show business has made regular school attendance impossible, and all through the years the children have been educated partly by correspondence courses and private tutors. Their family unit has been a great educator too — their inter-teaching of instrument skills is an example. Besides the inevitable "rubbing-off" process, similar teaching between parent or older brother and younger member has taken place in other areas of learning. Given the dedication and persistence which seems to be a family trait, it is conceivable that they have in this way obtained a better basic education than regular schools could have provided.

How does Marie see this experience? "We have tutors and correspondence courses, and traveling around the world itself is an education. You get to see the places that you would normally only read about, and that makes it really interesting. I know a lot of kids who don't think education is important and who don't want to make anything of themselves. They'll say, 'You're in show business, why do you want to study?' In other words, What do you need brains for? But I realize that it's good to have an education. It makes life more meaningful and gives you something to fall back on. It makes people respect you. I've heard my brothers say there's nothing worse than a dumb girl. They've really helped me in getting an education, and I really love school. I think the reason kids don't like school is that they don't understand the need for it. You have to get knowledge and develop your abilities. How can you compete in the world without them, or raise your children, or whatever?"

Important as they are, academics are only a small part of Marie's interests. She enjoys cooking, sewing, and embroidering, for instance. But today's statement on her activities would always be out of date tomorrow, for she has a zest for life which keeps her constantly busy in trying out new pursuits, learning new skills. All the while she pushes herself in the development of her singing and performing skills. When one achievement is completed, she's looking for another mountain to climb.

Beautiful, poised, friendly, self-assured beyond her years — yet sensitive and sometimes nervous in new situations. Confident, popular singer and performer who is modest about her accomplishments. Outgoing personality, fun to be with. Thoughtful, solid in character and conviction. And with all her talents, a down-home type of girl.

Mr. Right, wherever you are — you're a lucky man!

14   *Stands and Standards*

It's quite a while since those days of the early struggles —
the pinching of pennies to put a tour in the black, the
ever-present risk of indifferent supporting musicians, the
theater managers' unconcern about "just another" barbershop group, to say nothing of the homesickness and the
discomforts of "life on the road" away from home. Now
the Osmonds are at the top, that much-coveted position
which too frequently seems to bestow a commensurate
loftiness of attitude. How do the Osmonds respond to this
position? What changes would the observer notice since
the earlier years?

It may not make news, but the short answer is that
there has been no basic change. While the need to penny-
pinch is gone, the wisdom which prompted that course,
now shared by mature sons who are equal partners in the
family enterprise, still guides the family fortunes. There is
no ostentation of dress or lifestyle, and if you came face to
face with an Osmond on the street and did not know him
you would pass him by without comment. It's the same
with every other part of their lives, whether personal or
business. The reason is easy to see — if they had been
going to change, the time for this was on the way up, when
the pressures were on them, and not now.

Those who dream of having a million dollars and the ease it would bring forget that usually the man with the million learned the value of work in getting it and now could find no fulfillment without work. The type of labor may change. The Osmonds no longer get up early to milk a cow, hoe beets, stack bales of hay or whatever before a day's school which would be followed by singing practice, a nap, and an evening's performance. But work they do, and with as much zest as ever. "From early years they were self-motivators," says George. "They had to be, because Olive and I had to spend a great deal of time in helping Virl and Tom to communicate, and to a great extent the other boys had to dig for themselves."

They're still digging. From a conversation in the fall of 1974 comes this not untypical comment on the schedule of the songwriting trio, Alan, Wayne and Merrill. "We have to write four more songs for our album and a few more for Marie; a couple for Donny and Marie; and then some for a movie score." In what period? "We have about a month." There'd be a similar kind of schedule for Jay and Donny, with instrumental and vocal practice for them all. Not much fear of the work ethic being deserted in the Osmond clan.

There's no desire either to change their attitude toward the entertainment they purvey. That attitude springs from their simple philosophy that there are two forces in life, one good and the other evil, and that virtually anything in life can be used as a medium for either force. Usually the glitter and the sensual appeal of the negative force makes it the more immediately attractive — and that is the secret of its success and its addictive power. But the positive force lifts rather than degrades, promotes personal growth, harmonizes with life's higher aims. And these concepts apply to music as to any other art form.

As to personal likes, the brothers have fairly universal tastes in music. "Everyone's different," says Wayne, "and providing they are being moved in the right direction, people should go for that music that moves them inside. I can be thrilled by the brilliant composition and rendition of a symphony. And I can get excited too by a powerful choir — like the Mormon Tabernacle Choir. When I'm there I can feel the musical power of those hundreds of voices, and it's a very moving experience."

Coming closer to their own brand of music, what do they like there? Merrill's reply would be a fair summary for them all. "What's interesting about our music is that we like to do just about everything. We like playing Dixieland, we enjoy singing rhythm and blues, folk, country and western, love ballads — just about everything."

All this variety has to stand the test — their test. Which side of the line is it on? They recognize that with rock music they are in an area of controversy. "First of all," explains Alan, "we don't get into hard rock. The hard rock is extreme — very loud, and frequently it has suggestive lyrics and is performed with suggestive actions. Ours is a middle-of-the-road type of music, for easy listening."

But what about that beat? "Well, there's a 'beat' of sorts to every piece of music, from Bach's lilting 'Minuet in G' to the Beatles' driving 'Hey, Jude!' You can't have music without some kind of rhythm, and in modern music that rhythm is brought out by the beat. It's the speed, the emphasis, and the intensity of the beat that sets the mood of the music. There's something about the rock beat that makes people want to get up and dance; and so long as it's all clean and in fun there's nothing wrong with dancing."

The problem is, as the brothers realize, that a rock group beat can do more than impel a listener to dance.

More than one psychiatrist, in analyzing the situation, has concluded that rock groups do not realize the power of their rhythmic beat, an almost hypnotic power. "And it's true, too," Jay agrees. "We've been to some concerts ourselves, as part of the audience, that is. An audience can go in kind of excited to see a group perform, but it becomes more than excitement. The group just keeps on repeating that 'da-da-da-da-da-da-da-da,' and it's the repetition that gets people hypnotized. You can actually see them losing control — doing animalistic things, really. Now that's something our group doesn't provoke. The kids will get excited at our concerts, because that's what fans do, but our music doesn't induce them to lose self-control."

That beat may have a lot to answer for, for while, as someone has put it, "the music is the medium and the lyrics direct the path," it's the beat that grabs the attention. According to the conclusion of one psychiatrist, the hypnotic power of the beat makes sure the listener will in fact listen to the lyrics. And that in turn in the Osmonds' view puts a big responsibility not only on the performer but also on the writer of the lyrics.

Back in the sixties, here was the dilemma for the Osmonds: The top echelons in the field were giving the fans the extremes of hard rock, lyrics and all, and the whole atmosphere up there seemed to be part of the drug scene. The Osmonds would not pay that price for success, but their ambition impelled them to push for the top. They must find another way. Olive picks up the story:

"We could see that if you can get attention with the rhythm, you can drive home a message with the words. We were influenced in our thinking by something Art Linkletter said after his daughter got involved with the drug scene and committed suicide. He said, 'Let's give this generation their music, but let's put good lyrics with it, and then we might have something to solve the problem.' That's sort of what we've tried to do. The boys were getting nowhere singing and recording their soft pretty harmonies, and it wasn't until they came out with 'One Bad Apple' that they even got the attention of the youth. Then the young people began to say, 'Wow! Maybe the Osmonds have something.' That gave us a door-opener, and the boys started writing songs and came up with things like 'The Plan.' Then the kids would listen, but before that they wouldn't."

It's not necessarily an original idea, but the Osmonds believe there is far too much low-grade material around these days in the entertainment field generally. "The movies have drifted into it," Wayne comments, "the magazines too. As an example, a friend of ours asked the editor of one of the teen magazines, 'Why are you going in for this trashy element?' And he answered, 'Because that's what's selling.' It's a matter of commercialism, apparently — sell anything you can, regardless. But we didn't want to go along with that. Although it looked as if we were going out on a limb, we wanted to try to rescue the good while there was still some around."

In those earlier days of recording, before they got into gear in the songwriting area, they had plenty of temptation to bend their principles. "In many of the lyrics you could interpret meanings two ways," says Alan, "so we had to rewrite quite a few lyrics. But where that wasn't possible, we just had to turn the songs down altogether. We got a lot of pressure from recording companies. They'd say, 'It's not that bad,' or 'It doesn't mean that.' We probably lost a lot of money that way, but we didn't care."

The climax came when they were offered a song that everyone knew would be a hit but whose lyrics were unacceptable. Again the pressure, again the adamant position. Some other group recorded it, and sure enough it turned out to be a smash-hit. But about a month later the Osmonds recorded "One Bad Apple." At time of writing (early 1975) this is their biggest selling record — almost three million copies to date.

There have been other conflicts, other moments of decision. One time they went to the recording studio and actually recorded a song. "But we were all embarrassed. I suppose we hadn't given it enough thought before that. We said, 'We can't sing that.' Yet there were thousands of dollars already spent on that track."

The Osmonds phoned the writer of the lyrics, a Black, and he came to the studio. He was one of the top writers. The management said, "Don't ask him to change it. You'll blow it. That writer will never write for you again!" Nevertheless they explained their position to him.

"George and I sat opposite him and we talked," says Olive. " 'We know that whoever you give this song to you'll have a hit,' we told him, 'but the boys have made statements and they must follow up. They just can't go along with these words.' We knew he must have the opportunity of giving the song to some other star.

"He sat there for a moment looking at George, then he said, 'You remind me of my pappy down on the plantation. When I did something wrong he spanked me for it. And I deserved it.' Then he went right back out and changed the lyrics. We were most grateful for his kindness and consideration." He worked with Alan and the others, changing the words until they were completely satisfied.

The rerecorded song became a hit record. "If we had allowed it to go out as originally recorded, it would have meant that we were compromising," says Alan. "Most likely too it wouldn't have been a hit, because our followers know our stand and it would have let us down in their eyes."

For the Osmonds it's been stands and standards all the way. "But in any case," says Wayne, "it's much easier to write a trashy lyric, and we enjoy the challenge of writing one that's worthwhile." If they are careful about the cleanliness of their lyrics, they have been equally concerned about appearing with an act which was *not* careful in that way. "When we were second acts, we always had clauses in our contracts specifying that we didn't have to work on the same program with someone who was using dirty material." And they've turned down tours and lost money rather than work with such acts. "What another performer presents on his own is his business and not ours, but if we work with someone it looks as if we agree with the tone of his act and what he's saying."

Another standard they've tried to maintain is what they subscribe to as their law of health, and they will politely sustain their customs and convictions in this regard in all circumstances. During a trip to Japan, they were scheduled for a visit with members of the Japanese royal family. The booking agent who had arranged this had lived in Japan all his life, and he was overjoyed at this his first opportunity to enter the royal grounds. He explained to the Osmonds that there would be the customary simple but ritualistic ceremony with the royal family, which would involve drinking tea with cherry blossoms on the side. They would of course enjoy this delightful part of the experience.

There was one little detail he didn't know about. The Osmonds don't drink tea. Period. They explained that total abstinence from tea, coffee, tobacco and alcohol is part of their faith. Oh, but this was the royal family, the agent explained, and the Osmonds could not refuse this little ceremony. The visitors did not see it that way — "We have rights too," they would privately comment later. They asked if they could cancel the visit so as not to offend the royal family by not participating and thereby appearing disrespectful. But it was too late to cancel; everything had been arranged, and the family was waiting. They wanted to meet this Jimmy Osmond who was a favorite of the grandchildren in that family. The Osmonds recall that it was they who were treated royally. That day happened to be Jimmy's birthday and there was a huge hat for him — a warrior's helmet — and gifts for everybody. The head of the family, a bright, enlightened individual, was aware of his visitors' predicament by the time he greeted them, and when it came time for the tea ceremony the Osmonds were given bowls of warm water with the cherry blossom.

It's such a little thing, one might say, a small sip of tea. What's the difference? Who will it hurt? To the Osmonds these are not even the right questions. The question is rather: Since I've committed myself, why would I not follow through?

"Munich is the home of beer. Everybody drinks beer in Munich; therefore it's reasonable to assume everyone in Munich drinks Munich beer." This is the essence of an advertisement, and there is a great deal of truth to it. Hence the vivacious and lovely girl assigned as a guide to the Osmonds in Munich conceived it to be her first duty to take them to a famous restaurant noted for its 101 different beers.

As they were in the process of ordering their meal, nine steins of beer suddenly appeared on the table. Nine surprised looks promptly appeared around the table. The family appreciated the consideration, they told the guide, but could they please have something else — like apple juice.

"Oh, no!" the girl said, "you must taste our good Munich beer."

"We don't want to offend you, but we'd rather have apple juice," Alan responded, "or water's fine."

The girl insisted with a smile. "Just one sip. One sip couldn't possibly hurt you."

The Osmonds held firm even as a little irritation crept into the girl's manner. They answered her softly, and shortly they were enjoying good Munich apple juice.

The next day the newspaper headline read: "Osmonds Prefer Apple Juice to Munich Beer." "Suppose it said, 'Osmonds Enjoy Munich Beer,' " muses Alan. "We would have felt we'd let down the folks back home as well as ourselves."

If many fellow-performers think them a little strange for the insistence on clean material, they probably think they're nuts for their attitude toward Sunday. In all their frequently hectic, always busy life, the Osmonds have preserved a haven in this one day of the week. With only one or two exceptions as regards personal appearances, when contractually there was no alternative, they have refused to work on Sundays, either in personal appearances, recordings, rehearsing, songwriting, or anything connected with show business — for that matter, any weekday pursuits. Even some of their managers, as close as they were to the group, have not understood that they were "in concrete" on this issue. "They'd say to us, 'Look, you're paying your own transportation for a weekend job when you only work Friday and Saturday. Don't you realize that when you go to a place like Seattle, if you'd work Sunday that would pay for your transportation, and you'd have the take from Friday and Saturday clear?' "

The mathematics of this were clear to the group long before the manager put the proposition. But they feel they have good reasons for their stand. "We need to rest one day in seven, as everyone else does. And we need to go to church and recharge our spiritual batteries. That's what the Lord's day is all about."

Those batteries get a fillip or two on other days as well, for the singing Osmonds are also praying Osmonds — they pray as a group before every performance. What do they pray for? "Well, of course we're not asking for some miraculous power to descend on us and make us super-performers," explains Alan. "We're not asking to get out more than we've put in, and humanly speaking we're already well prepared. But we ask for help to do our best, to recall readily what we've learned in rehearsals, to be in control of the situation on stage. I believe we'd sooner go on stage minus an instrument than minus the strength the prayer gives us. We've never done one performance without it." It wasn't always easy to find an appropriate place, either. They remember one state fair where their prayer was offered in the corner of a tent while understanding officials courteously kept people away.

They recall too a prayer in an interesting situation. Habitually they pray for protection before leaving for an engagement, but as mortals will they have occasionally overlooked this in the rush to get away. One day in the early years, when one car would accommodate performers, costumes, props and lunch sacks, they had not long left home when someone remembered the prayer. George pulled off the road and he and the boys bowed their heads. The chosen spot happened to be just short of the entrance to the Los Angeles freeway.

As they sat there immobile, a motorcycle policeman pulled up behind them. From the posture of the occupants he was sure something must be wrong, so he tapped sharply on the driver's window. He was relieved to see all the heads come up at the same time. George rolled down the window, told him that everything was fine, and explained in a matter-of-fact way that they were just offering up a prayer. The officer put both hands on the edge of the car, looked at those five smiling faces, and said, "I wish more people would do that before they venture out on these freeways."

Well, that's the Osmonds. They haven't changed their standards along the way and they certainly don't plan on it for the future. For them it seems to be paying off in their own measure of success. "We've found that the crowds we play to are good, mostly wholesome-type kids. We don't have much of the other element — those who're on pot and drugs and all that stuff — because they think we're 'square.' But more and more we seem to be attracting the young people to what we believe is the better way."

Merrill picks up where his father left off. "More than that, the people who I guess you could say are making that other scene have a respect for us. They may not believe what we believe (though sometimes I get the impression they'd like to) but they can't put us down, because at least we're trying to stand for our beliefs. They recognize that that's not easy. In fact, a reporter of one of the more extreme magazines, after an interview with Alan, said, 'Hey, you know, you guys are all right.' "

And how about that other measure of achievement, the world's? They don't set too much store by that. "It's trite but true," says Alan — and he couldn't be more clearly speaking for the group — "that you can't take it with you. It's your personality that you take with you."

In case you should press the point, you might question the financial effect of some of their decisions, even ask them to assess how much money they lost by their policy on Sunday work, clean material, and so on. They'll surprise you by saying that overall they've actually gained money. "We rest on Sunday, and we have sharper brains for songwriting on Monday. It's the same with other areas. There's a law of compensation so that somehow you eventually profit in every way by holding to right principles. It's certainly worked for us."

As the colloquialism has it, "You'd better believe it." You'll have a hard time arguing with the Osmonds — or with their success.

Jimmy had been working on this recording for over two hours. He was tired; you could see the weariness in his young face. Not that he was tired of the family criticisms, for his brothers have the ability to criticize him and lift him at the same time. He knew the pattern, for he had seen them evaluate each other's performance many times — no bluntness or sharpness, yet a quickness to point out short-comings for the good of the team, all feeling free to critique each other.

"Watch that last phrase, now." "You're still slur-ring that word a little." "That's the boy, Jimmy!" Each time it meant recording another portion of the song. Then the family would listen carefully to the complete tape or a suspect portion. That too might result in further retaping. And so on. But Jimmy was not concerned. It was no sur-prise to him that his family are perfectionists in their approach to their art.

All the while Donny had been at the control panel, alternating between getting the song "laid down" on tape and joining in the family's assistance to Jimmy. Finally he raised his right hand and made a circle with his thumb and forefinger. A three-minute song had been completed, a song which from first note to last had taken three hours.

Jimmy's bubbly effervescence permeates the atmosphere during "showtime," whether live or in recording, but away from the spotlights he has his quiet, reflective moments. "When I was younger — it was right before we went to Sweden — I was never happy, and I always had a big frown on my face. Even the funniest things — I'd laugh at 'em at the time, but right away I'd get serious again. It's kinda like Marie — she remembers Father taking her over to a corner and straightening her out. Well, Father began spending more time on me — I suppose you could say he disciplined me. Anyway, things kinda straightened out."

The recollection of this experience gives rise to some youthful philosophizing. "I see lotsa kids going around with a big frown plastered all over their face. You'd think they'd all been eating dill pickles for breakfast. Maybe they're not happy with what they have in life. There sure are lotsa wicked things going on today, but what's worst of all is to hear the news on TV. I think the news should be X-rated. All they have is bad news. I'd like to see something good or funny. But I guess if the world's in such a sad state, maybe there isn't any good news. I think we'd all better start doing something right for a change."

As an Osmond, Jimmy's helping to bring the world a little cheer. Any book about the Osmonds' current level of skills would be out of date before it was published, but at time of writing (early 1975), as well as singing and dancing, Jimmy is learning to play the trombone, and with that instrument he joins the group in a Dixieland sequence they have going. Jay is teaching him to play the drums — and to ride a unicycle. He's continually surprised at his brothers' proficiency on their various instruments. He soon realized that you just didn't pick up an instrument

James Arthur Osmond

and hold it while it played itself. As with his brothers before him, he set about learning the fundamentals. He's not afraid to try something new, and is remarkably graceful of movement on stage. If you watch him with his brothers you can readily see how he emulates them — a prominent feature of this musical group. Like the others before him, Jimmy will give it all he's got. He has a tremendous reserve of energy, and frequently when the rest of the brothers are in the last stages of exhaustion following a practice or performance, he's still going strong.

What does he like to do besides perform? Well, he still clings to portions of the little boy — cowboys and Indians, model cars, rocket launchers, airplanes. He enjoys physical pursuits — baseball, tennis, basketball, golf, cycling, horseback riding. When it comes to sports, he has Jay's tendencies. Yet he can sit quietly and read, and he enjoys painting. His style of talking is somewhat more mature than most of those of his age — naturally, since he's been around adults a great deal and has patterned his speech after theirs.

"Father turned my sour face around when we started doing more things together. Since I've been traveling I've learned a lot and I get to see things that other kids don't. You know, we have an advantage there, and I really appreciate it. Most kids would give their right arm to do what I do and see what I see. I hope I don't ever get to a point where I can't appreciate those things any more. My family makes it fun and important for me. I've been to the Orient, to Europe, all over the Scandinavian countries. It's fun — although of course it wouldn't be without my family."

Some of Jimmy's fun and excitement have come from his experiences in Japan. Japanese food, for instance. "We all went to a restaurant there, and we had to eat with

Young man
of varied interests

At the mike

chopsticks. It was quite a problem. The food looked something like spaghetti and meat balls, and there was loads of
it. It was really yummy, too. But after we'd eaten it they
told us it was jellyfish tentacles or shark-fin soup, and
things like that."

Ask Jimmy his impression of that kind of food and
you'll get a half-diplomatic answer. "I guess it's a matter of
developing a taste for it." He'll confide that right now good
old American hamburgers are fine with him.

Jimmy's talents and youthful innocence stole the
hearts of the Japanese people, and with his kind of celeb-
rity status he was a "natural" for a nation-wide TV commercial. It was a soft-drink firm that scooped him up, and
taping the various commercials took him to many different
places — Hawaii, Acapulco, Denver, and many more. The
commercial was shown on TV in Japan almost every day
for five years.

At eleven, Jimmy came into the possession of an
electronic experimental and testing kit, and Donny — the
Marconi-Edison-Bell of the family — is teaching him the
fundamentals. "Donny and I usually room together when
we're on tour, and occasionally we have to be locked in
and there's nobody but the two of us. So he lets me talk a
lot. It kinda gets my mind off the fact that we can't go
outside except to go on stage. When we get back home we
can circulate without anyone paying any attention to us.
That's a nice feeling."

Jimmy hastens to add that in saying this he's not
knocking show business. That's too exciting a life. "It's a
strange feeling to go out on stage, and I don't know if I can
describe it. When I'm backstage I'm really shaking all over,
but then right when I step on stage I don't feel a thing. I see
all the people out there, but I've lost that urge to run away

and hide. Then I can feel the strength of my brothers, so I get the calmest feeling, and it lasts until I get off stage."

Jimmy gives an interesting, boy's-eye view of what happens after the show. "Later in the car, when we leave the theater, the windows get all steamed up and my brothers pick out the bad things we did on stage. They call it evaluation. They just get in the car and 'rip off,' and that way we usually improve our act. I think it's important to keep improving. Alan says that if we ever get perfect, we probably won't be here any more. I've got an idea of what he means by that."

How does Jimmy relate to other youngsters his own age? Ask him that, and you'll get a mixture of anecdote and philosophy. Once when attending public school in Huntsville, Utah, he acquired a friend who was known to other children as an "oddball." This youngster didn't wear the updated clothing the others did, and he rarely joined in group activity. Yet there was something about him that drew Jimmy to him. "I really liked him, because you could always talk to him and he seemed to understand." Jimmy sensed behind those sad eyes the longing to belong, to be like the others, to be accepted. Yet as is often the case in the young set, subtle cruelties were being inflicted upon him as an "outsider"; he must either learn to adjust or run away and hide. Jimmy's friend was trying to bridge the gap in his own peer group, and while Jimmy had no problems himself in this respect, he could empathize with someone who did.

He had another friend in that school, a teacher. She was "a really nice lady," and he could talk to her too. As a new student he was called an unflattering name by a classmate — a not unusual situation when a new and popular person enters a class and perhaps threatens the established "pecking order." Clearly the young Mr. Osmond was soak-

In the family studio – ready to record

ing up some of the adulation which had, until recently, been directed toward the other student.

The "nice lady" asked the young man to apologize for his inconsideration. She knelt down to speak on his level and he greeted her with a roundhouse to the nose. This blatant show of youthful frustration upset Jimmy. With his training in showing respect for adults, he just couldn't understand that reaction. "How could he do that?" he asks.

That same youngster had a penchant for peering at other students' papers during class tests. Aware of what was going on, the teacher took the wise and tactful course — she told the whole class that every time someone's eyes strayed from his own paper his grade would be lowered. But the message intended for the one fell upon deaf ears and she finally had to send the troubled youngster to the principal.

When school let out that day, instead of going home the students from that class waited restlessly in the playground. While they may have resented the cheating, they had some concern for the cheat. Two hours after being admitted to the principal's office he emerged, white-faced and red-eyed. When his friends tried to quiz him he burst past them and ran for the sanctuary of his home.

Someone was in trouble, and although he had tried to make himself an "enemy," Jimmy's sympathies were again enlisted. "I really wanted to say something to him, but I didn't know what to say — and before I could say anything he'd gone anyway." The boy never returned during Jimmy's stay in school.

The incident left a profound impression on Jimmy. "You know, even if I was just kinda raising my head to think about a question on a test, I remember how quickly I would lower it again if I caught a glimpse of a piece of paper on somebody's desk." The episode stayed with him and reinforced his already strong belief in the principle of honesty.

By the time Jimmy came on the scene, his brothers were established stars and were busy with their careers. "They really worked hard and I guess I came along when they had it made." But he knew that if he were to become a part of the act he had to learn how. His brothers were always patient and understanding in their approach to him. "Whenever I get a line wrong when we're rehearsing or recording, they just have me do it again. They never have jumped on me because I've flubbed. We've never started a show or TV special or anything without first praying for help to do our best; so I guess when they ask for help like that, it's easy for them to understand that I need help too." His brothers' help has paid off right from the start. Jimmy, the youngest, had the first gold record in the family — "My Little Darling."

Jimmy has his own room where he can be alone. "I can get out my little black-and-white TV and hibernate like a bear." The room contains a small bench where he can do leather work. Like Donny, he enjoys sleeping up near the ceiling, so his bed is built up there and he enters the "bed compartment" by a trap door. Neat, eh? He thinks so.

"Neater" still is his "cave," which is guarded by a piece of plywood. "It's really small, but when you get up in the front of it, you can sit down. I put the TV outside my 'cave' and turn on my favorite cartoons and 'hibernate.' "

He also finds the "cave" an ideal place to do his school work. He enjoys the challenge the tutors place before him and he is a better-than-average student. One of

Plywood trap door covers entrance to Jimmy's "den" beside bed

But there's another entrance (or is it an exit?)

Now it's just a route to Jimmy's bed

the advantages of individualized teaching is that the student can progress at his own rate. "I guess school work's like food, not everybody likes the same stuff. I like science and geography and I'm not all that crazy about English. Course, I like pizza and chicken but I'm not wild about those 'sotic' dishes. But I guess I like club sandwiches most of all, cuz Donny and I can take out those little swords that hold 'em together and have a little sword fight." He glances off into space. "Sure like club sandwiches."

He sits back for a moment and observes the crease in his pants. Someone puts a record on the stereo. He runs his thumb and forefinger down the crease. "I think black pants are really classy." He begins to feel the rhythm and picks it up with a light bobbing of the head. "You know, I don't like heavy rock. It's too confusing. Sometimes they gotta lot of horrible sounds going on at the same time."

He begins to accentuate the beat with a pushing motion of his body. "That man singing right there is Stevie Wonder. He's my favorite. I love his voice, and it's amazing how he can play the piano so well without seeing it. He's a very neat guy."

The phrase is apt. James Arthur Osmond himself is a very neat guy.

"The Osmonds speak to youth," someone said. Well, they certainly speak to *some* youth through their music, their lyrics, their fan club, the Osmond Foundation. And they *like* to speak to youth. Through the thousands of letters they receive every month they get a pretty good measure of the major interests of young people. What better opportunity to speak to them than through this chapter?

For this purpose they are presently gathered in the spacious living room of the Osmond home, under Donny's thirty-two-light O for Osmond, relaxing on the large white semi-circular couch or on other sofas and chairs around the room. They are a group of formidable size, considerable experience, and pronounced opinions. At this point five of the sons are married, some rather recently. The other three boys and Marie are not. Naturally there's strong interest in the subject of marriage and what leads up to it — topics high on the list of fans' concerns too. It's a "rap" session, and questions and comments fly back and forth. Someone proposes a corker: What's the most central factor to a person in insuring a successful marriage?

Choosing the right person? Dating habits? Home organization? Family relationships? These and other possibilities come out. It's Wayne who provides the convincing answer. "Surely the most important thing is to *be* the right person. These other matters won't then be too much of a problem."

That sounds easy, but how is it achieved? "That's the tough part," Merrill concedes. "We were lucky to have parents who trained us right and set us a fine example, and even then we're not exactly angels. But we've always known what we were expected to be and what to look for in a partner. How about all those kids out there who're groping for the answers, who haven't yet found *themselves*, let alone found the basis for selecting that special person?"

Tough, all right! "It's hard for us even to comprehend the problem, because we haven't had the experience." Heads nod in agreement with Alan's words. "But we've known many people who have, and some of them we've been able to help. Remember those two Jewish girls, for example, how they used to follow our group around? Remember how bitter and cutting they were at first? But they came out of it — actually found an entirely new and happy life. So perhaps we can help when people contact us. After all, a doctor doesn't have to have had a particular disease in order to help cure it in a patient."

So what would the doctor prescribe in this situation? No problem in getting suggestions here. They boil down basically to a lifting of mental attitude. Take an affirmative approach to life. Have faith in the rightness of things. Look up, not down. Fill the mind and time with good and progressive things, worthy company. Set good goals. Find life's purpose and make it an ally. When you stumble, get up and press on again. In time you'll become that right person and will recognize that rightness in someone else.

Donny brings up what is a very practical matter for

every teen-ager. "I think one of the problems is that kids get too impatient — they can't wait to date, so they get at it too early. I believe it's important to wait till you're sixteen before you date. I know I looked forward to it, but if I'd been allowed to go out with girls when I was fourteen or so, I wouldn't have been mature enough — I'd probably have done something dumb that would have taken the glow off the whole thing. And anyway, the purpose of dating is to eventually find an eternal companion, and until you're about sixteen you don't have good enough judgment even for the early stages of that search."

Marie puts it another way. "I think when you're sixteen you're more adult. The years before that you get mentally ready for dating."

Amid murmurs of approval comes Jay's "I didn't date till I was sixteen, and I don't think I missed a thing."

Merrill follows that one up. "Kids only think they may be missing something when they're looking ahead to dating. But it's not that big of a deal. A year or two in the early teens is neither here nor there, and there's lots more to do anyway."

"That's what's great about growing up and becoming sixteen." George gets into the act now. "In a way you're off on your own. You're grown up enough to be out there, but there's no pressure to talk about serious things. You're just having fun. Sixteen, seventeen, eighteen — they're the starting-out years. You have to savor them."

"They can be dangerous years too," Olive responds. "Many youngsters get on the wrong track morally during that period."

As the Osmond currently in that age bracket, Donny has another word to say here. "We've talked to lots of kids

Preparing the
monthly teen
magazine –

The family
discusses
material
for inclusion

Olive roughs
out an article

Family members enjoy
talking with young people

who've been caught up in that kind of life — an immoral relationship. When they come out of it they always tell us they regret it. They tell us they've lost respect for the other person and also for themselves, that it just wasn't worth it. I guess they were looking for their fun in the wrong way. I get my fun with a girl doing simple things — listening to music, sharing our hobbies, going to a good movie or dance, swimming, throwing a beachball, going to a church function, or just sitting around talking. Most of the time I double date anyway, because it's more enjoyable that way. I have lots of fun with many different girls, and I don't have any regrets."

Now Mary chips in. "Having fun is a big part of it. That's what's so silly about going steady during those years. In high school I never wanted to go steady — I was having so much fun going out with different boys. But everyone else seemed to be going steady, and there was a lot of social pressure to do it. I gave in for a time, and while I kept going out with this guy I'd lecture myself — 'You're going to like going with him all the time because it's the thing to do.' I finally quit, and I felt very good about that. But I think girls especially tend to hang on in those circumstances. 'Am I going to find that knight in shining armor? If not, I'd better grab the next best thing.' That's a good way to start a marriage headed for the rocks."

Merrill squeezes his wife's hand as she finishes. "Dating is a prelude to selecting a permanent partner, and you don't do much selecting if you're always with the same person. Even in choosing a date I've tried to be selective. I'd often say to myself, 'Would I marry a girl with those qualities?' We do marry someone we date."

"Right." It's Alan again. "Before I got married I had a pretty thick little black book. I recall frequently thumbing through it and saying, 'No! Perhaps. Maybe. No!' It was

sort of an initial selection process in the search for an
eternal partner — and, of course, any girl I asked for a date
was entitled to accept or not on the same kind of basis.

"I found that the type of date varied quite a bit.
Some people feel they have to impress somebody on a
date, and I don't like that — it's not relaxed. Some girls
expect you to kiss them on the first date; some don't want
you to, and I believe that's the right thing. (I dated Suzanne
for a long time before I kissed her.) The best dates I've had
was where we'd do simple things, even crazy things sometimes — on the beach, for example. You don't have to
spend a lot of money, you don't have to try to impress
anybody. You just be yourself. Talk about mutual interests, play a game together — like tennis, or whatever."

"Trouble is, my girls won't play football with me,"
Jay laughs. "And, you know, just to watch her expression, I
sometimes say to a girl I'm dating, 'Do you kiss on the first
date?' If she says no, I ask, 'How about the last date?' "

As the laughter subsides, Kathy gets in. "The thing
is, you'd better not compromise your values in selecting
your companion. You'd better not just grab someone and
decide that after marriage you'll make him or her over to
suit you. We're all too set in our ways and our standards to
be remade by others, and a lot of people get very disil-
lusioned with marriage when they try this and fail."

"Since we're back on the serious side," Wayne in-
terjects, "let me throw this one in. We like to think in terms
of 'you're the only one in the world for me,' but really I
wonder about that. If we date someone and we're compat-
ible, we have similar interests, and we come to like that
person a lot, we can perhaps learn to love him or her. Some
of my friends are twenty-eight or twenty-nine and still
unmarried, yet they've dated some fine girls. They're wait-

ing for the bell, but it doesn't quite ring; so they don't make the effort to find out if that's the person they should marry."

"Also," Suzanne comments, "you need to cut it off if you can see that that person is not right for you. It's harder on both of you if you just keep kidding yourselves along, and it's not really fair to the other person. I dated some fine fellows who had a lot of the qualities I was looking for. But it didn't click. I had to move on, and I knew that someday I'd find him. I prayed a lot about it, and I felt confident that the Lord would lead me to the right person. Of course, we have to remember that we ourselves are not perfect, so we won't expect to find a perfect companion. Also, we have to make the best of ourselves. Sometimes it's a weight problem, or a skin problem, or how we carry ourselves. I suppose we should say to ourselves, 'Well, would you want to marry someone who looks like you?' and if the answer is positive, we're at least on the right track."

"I'm glad you brought that up." Jay is serious now. "Nobody is without some kind of a problem, or at least something they'd like to change. It's a matter of building faith and confidence in yourself and being reasonably presentable with what you have. A person doesn't have to be a side-show event to get the proper attention. But kids nowadays are so fashion conscious that they forget their personalities, and their dating becomes phony because they're trying to impress. Sure, you're supposed to look good because that's where the other person is going to get his interest, but after that it's up to your personality, what you are inside."

"And that's too often the problem, as I see it," Olive reflects, "especially with girls. Too many think that looks and clothes are everything, and they sit at home pining their lives away instead of making something of their lives that would attract others to them. They should participate socially, get involved in programs at church, school or work, develop a talent in some field. Then they will attract others of similar interest and caliber, and eventually they'll find the right one."

"And live happily ever after!" Jay is in a puckish mood again.

George has to get in on that one. "Well, now, that depends on a lot of factors. For instance, what do the couple think about marriage itself? Do they see it basically as a permanent relationship or do they look at it as something easy to escape from through divorce?"

Virl's quiet voice is heard. "Do they even believe in getting married in the first place? So many don't today."

There is a general hush at this remark. The thought is almost sacrilegious to the Osmonds, to whom marriage is not merely the only proper arrangement under which a man and woman may live together in physical intimacy but is also a cardinal principle of the Christian religion. Any such intimacy outside of marriage is wrong. Period. This includes intimacy short of the procreative act itself. On the other hand, marriage is ordained of God, and within that relationship the expression of mutual love in the procreative act is likewise divinely approved. In show business in particular there can be a lot of temptations to immorality. "But there's never an acceptable reason for letting down your moral standards, and secretly people will admire you if you don't. Unless you try to live a moral life you can't build mutual respect and trust with your partner and you can't raise your children properly."

Old-fashioned? An out-moded morality? A naive

ignorance of the progressive modern lifestyle embodying the "new morality"? As you will. The Osmonds won't argue with you. But they act as if they know whereof they speak, and they are not about to be made over.

Some facets of the matters under discussion are subject to differing opinions in the group, but this one is not. "I guess we could say that for all of us marriage is meant to be stable, permanent, enduring forever. We wish everyone would look at it in this way. Society would then be a lot more stable because there'd be a lot less divorces and a lot more happy families."

Families. That's another question. With nine children, the Osmonds have what the world would call a "large" family. Can such a family be justified in an era of the pill, the easy abortion, the "population explosion"?

"Absolutely," says Tom. "Larger families are happier — at least, that's our experience. Both the parents and the children learn unselfishness and cooperation, and that has to make things happier. Anyway, I don't go for the modern reasoning. It's offering man-made solutions to man-made problems — and both the problem and the solution are wrong."

"I've read that overall there's no population explosion that can't be handled," Jay recalls.

"And that's right," Alan confirms. "There is much unused, habitable space on the earth. And there's a far larger potential of food supply than the world produces. We read of politics, graft and laziness preventing underdeveloped countries from learning to feed themselves despite many years of assistance from abroad. In our own land, mismanagement has reduced large food supplies to shortages. Men blame nature instead of themselves for masses of starving people, then they propose remedies that are against all nature. It's not a population explosion that's the real problem. It's the failure of men and governments to organize, cooperate, share, and generally get along together.

"But it's a lot easier to blame nature than to change people, so along comes man-made solutions — restrict families by contraception and abortion. Both solutions are wrong — morally wrong. Like our parents, this generation of Osmonds proposes to have all the children the good Lord will send us. And we know that, if we work hard, he'll help us provide for them and raise them, as he will any other parents who ask for his help."

The words *parents* and *generation* bring to some of the assembled minds another modern term, "generation gap." It's the wife of one of the brothers who speaks the phrase. The Osmonds have never experienced a generation gap, but through personal contacts and letters from fans they are very conscious of its existence. What causes it? Olive leads out on this one.

"I'm sure there are lots of reasons, but it's the breakdown of the true family life that has to take most of the blame. I understand that the generation gap doesn't exist in some Oriental countries, where strong family ties are still the norm. But individual families can still hold the line in America and other western countries if they go about it in the right way. Parents need to show genuine love for their children as they grow up — discipline them, yes, but let them know they are loved. Even in families that are having problems, I don't believe it's too late to start over if both the parents and the young people will admit their mistakes and be forgiving.

"I must say that when difficulties arise I don't feel that it is always the young person's fault. Parents too are sometimes quite rigid and don't make allowances for modern trends even where it wouldn't hurt a thing to do so."

"Like in music," Marie suggests.

"Yes, music's one area," her mother responds. "I'll admit that I still prefer the sweeter, softer melodies and harmonies of the thirties and the forties. It's as if you always prefer the music of your youthful days, and I remember that when I was young the older generation preferred the music of the twenties and earlier. But I can take some of the less extreme music of today too. In fact, some of the music of the past, even some of the classics, can be quite dreary and depressing and can make you feel down in spirit, whereas a good bouncy tune on the radio in the morning can perk you right up and set you in gear for the day."

Music is a subject all the family could discuss at length. Merrill picks it up. "That's one thing about you and Father — you were always willing to listen to a song and judge it on its merits. When the group began to phase out of barbershop and into more modern styles, you went along. You didn't cut off from us because the new style was different and perhaps not quite such pleasant listening for you."

Marie speaks up. "When parents resent the music the kids enjoy, that's bound to set up a barrier. The kids will then spend more and more time with their friends listening to that music. Lots of kids have found their way into drugs in that way, as they got caught up by the hard rock type of music. Sometimes perhaps it would have been different if the parents could have shared some of the modern music with them in the beginning and kept close to them in that way. I think it's bad when adults just out-and-out resent all the younger generation's music."

Jimmy has been itching to say a word, and now it pops out in a comment wise beyond his years. "I think parents and children would get a little closer to each other if they'd each try to understand the other generation's music. We kids ought to listen to the older generation's music. I like some of that music — it's good. And parents could understand their children better if they'd just try to 'dig' a little of our music."

"Right," says Alan, "so long as we remember that there's certainly a lot of modern music and lyrics that everyone ought to steer clear of — youth and adults."

"Well, isn't it the same way with clothes?" Virl's wife Chris has a word here. "Not all the modern styles are objectionable, but a lot are."

This is an area in which Tom's wife Lyn has strong feelings. "The major problem is a matter of modesty and decency, especially in girls' clothing. That ought to be the first consideration. Revealing clothes are temptations to immorality. It's as simple as that."

"That's true," says Olive, "and everyone knows it, though they won't all admit it. But there are differing style possiblities even in modest dress. Our family didn't have much difficulty in this area, since it's mainly girls' clothes that are affected, and we had only one girl. But I think my generation has its own idea about styles, and we frequently act as if no other way could be acceptable. So we look at a modern style and think, 'Wow! That's ugly, that's horrible!' But our children, looking back on our day and the clothes we wore, say 'Mother, how could you ever have worn anything that looks like that?' So maybe we ought to be a little more broadminded on this matter of our children's dress styles, so long as they properly cover the subject, so to speak."

That in this chapter the Osmonds have properly covered the subjects, the major subjects, which concern young people of today, is something they would not for a moment claim. They could have said much more on every topic raised. Similarly, opposing views could encompass volumes. But debating the issues was not their intent, and they have at least made clear for those who are interested what their views are on these matters.

From Father George Osmond down to young Jimmy, the Osmonds all relate well to youth. They genuinely believe that the youth of this world have a great potential for good, not merely as tomorrow's leaders and citizens but right now in their own homes and communities. And while they recognize that individual circumstances may often be discouraging, they point to men and women who have risen above poor or mediocre environment to achieve success and happiness in life by strong endeavor and a positive, uplifting philosophy of life.

You can do it! That's their faith in you, the young people of the world.

17   *Virl and Tom*

"I have a thousand songs I would like to sing. I'd like to hear the sound of a meadowlark. I'm curious to know whether a brook really babbles. What must the gentle rustle of leaves sound like? But most of all, I'd love to hear the soft cooing noises of my baby."

To the casual onlooker, Thomas Rulon Osmond is just like the good-looking young man next door; and until you notice that he is wearing hearing aids, you would take him for a young business executive, which he is, or a college student, which he was. But Tom Osmond is also deaf — hard deaf. Only about 10 percent of the sounds around us get through to him. "I will never forget how hard it was to say "cow." I was elated just to add another word to my list. My mother and father patiently put in countless hours helping me to speak, and I'm tremendously grateful to them."

Being an Osmond, Tom is blessed with the family musical talents. "In my mind I have a strong desire to be able to sing someday. In my travels I sing everywhere I go. I'm sure there are people who look at me, stopped at a traffic signal, or moving slowly from place to place in my car, and wonder what I must be doing, tapping on the steering wheel, bobbing my head, and moving my mouth.

They probably say, 'Huh, another nut's loose.' But I don't mind. I sing everywhere I go!''

Lest any should ungraciously wonder what Tom has to sing about, let it be known that underneath the hearing aids and the not-quite-normal speech is an exceptional self-sustaining individual. At the deaf school he was the only one in his graduating class to be awarded a graduating diploma instead of just a certificate of completion. An Eagle Scout like his brother Virl, he graduated from high school and went on to studies at the university. Modest, poised and friendly, he is a quick, perceptive person with the same positive attitude the entire family has.

Another thing he shares with them is a great sense of rhythm. When Tom and Virl were learning to tap dance, the teacher told Olive: "Virl picks it up because he watches my feet and he can imitate any move I make. Tom picks it up because he can feel the rhythm and the vibration of the music. I don't know which is the best way to get it." Regardless of the best way, get it they did, and these two oldest brothers were dancing long before the performing brothers put on their first tap shoes. Tom and Virl in fact taught the rest of the boys to dance.

When Lyn Heslop first saw Tom at a weekend dance at the University of Utah she was impressed. Obviously he was the best dancer on the floor. But to Lyn that wasn't all. "I was standing on one side of the room and he was on the other. I looked over at him and he seemed to be standing above everybody. He sort of stood out. When I looked at him I had the neatest feeling come over me, and the only person I can explain that special feeling to is someone who's had that same feeling when they've looked at someone."

When Tom finally asked Lyn to dance, she was

Tom on a scooter

With Lyn and son Benjamin

With Donny in
the printing shop

thrilled. While Lyn is by no means the possessor of two left feet, she did not move with the dexterity and skill of this Nijinsky, so after one dance he thanked her and went off in search of Pavlova.

Through the remainder of that school year the two ran across each other on several occasions and soon became good friends. That friendship grew into love, and Tom and Lyn were married in the Salt Lake Temple in January 1972, almost a year after that first dance.

Virl, the oldest brother, is not as profoundly deaf as Tom — about 40 percent deaf. Like the other brothers, he is musically gifted. In earlier days both he and Tom performed with the group, took music lessons right along with the others, appeared on Andy Williams shows, Phyllis Diller shows and others, tap dancing and playing the saxophone. But as the group progressed into more versatile onstage activities, a wider range of vocal and instrumental effort, Virl and Tom felt themselves to be falling behind, despite the help and encouragement of the hearing brothers. Even so, the decision to withdraw from the performing group was their own. The way was smoothed for that decision by the two older boys going on a two-year mission for their Church (Tom being the first deaf missionary sent out), during which time there was no opportunity to follow a musical career. When they got back, Donny had firmly established himself with the singing group. Shortly Virl and Tom got married.

A chance remark Virl made when he was twelve caused his mother to start him and Tom on tap dancing, saxophone and piano. It was the barbershop days; the boys had been out singing and were on their way home. Wrapped up in a blanket between George and Olive, Virl said gently, quietly, and almost unconsciously, "Gee, I wish I had some talent." The remark struck Olive deeply.

The next day she started Virl and Tom on saxophone lessons.

This development was to cause some friction between Olive and the school for the deaf which Tom was attending. The school had had some problems with her before. When she had wanted Tom to learn sign language they had objected, though they finally gave in. But now music lessons, dance lessons! How could this type of training possibly be of benefit to the deaf? Olive was a bit ahead of her time. Music and dance are now part of the curriculum for the deaf.

Among Olive's other differences of opinion with the school was her buying of good hearing aids for Virl and Tom as soon as these became available. "You're throwing your money away," they told her. "You people don't make that kind of money and you can't afford to waste it." It wasn't wasted. Virl's and Tom's abilities to speak and communicate well today are partly the result of just such "obstinacy" on George and Olive's part.

There are other solid reasons basic to the two brothers themselves. George calls it determination, persistence. "They've never let anything get them down — no handicaps, no problems, nothing. No matter how depressed they might become, it was temporary. They rose above it. They were fighters." Gentle, kind, but still fighters. There are several words which describe this quality. Perhaps the best one is *courage*.

As a boy, Tom so much wanted to be able to talk to develop his vocabulary that he would carry a small dictionary with him wherever he went. When he heard a new word, he'd look it up.

Olive deliberately refrained from learning sign language. "I thought Tom got enough of it at school, and I

Virl and his world of the family

wanted him to be able to hear enough, through the hearing aid, that he could communicate with those who couldn't." That is exactly what Tom has done, for now, like Virl, he does not need to use the sign language on his own account, but both these older brothers remain completely proficient at it and can interpret for deaf people. The other brothers know the sign language somewhat, but not with that kind of proficiency. They use it principally to communicate backstage when a show is in progress and they can't shout to each other.

Virl married Chris Carroll two months after he met her. "I knew it was right, so I didn't see any need for a long engagement." They met in California on a Sunday, in the church foyer. It was October, the day the clocks were set back at the end of daylight saving time. But both Virl and Chris had forgotten to reset their watches, and by this apparent coincidence, as Chris says, "Providence stepped in and placed us in each other's presence." They were married in the Los Angeles Temple in December 1968.

Like the other girls the brothers have married, Chris is an integral part of the family organization. Every month she answers several hundred letters from fans on religious questions alone. Do Mormons have more than one wife at a time? Do you believe in divorce? What's wrong with abortion? Are Mormons Christians? What's wrong with coffee and tea? She trys to make the answers honest, effective and personal.

Virl's and Tom's handicap may have kept them from the performing team but never from the closeness of the larger unit. The development of their interests was an asset here. Photography is prominent on the list of Tom's and Virl's hobbies, and with the attainment of professional skills they have become photographers for the group. As you visit in the Osmond home, more than likely Tom will come into the kitchen or the living room and snap an informal picture of Marie or Donny or some other family member. Alternatively chief family photographer Virl will shoot the pictures in his studio. From Virl's file of thousands he supplies most of the group's pictures for magazines, including those for the fan magazine.

The Osmond fan magazine is a total family effort, with Virl as the art director and production manager. And added to this area of their lives, and Tom's ownership of a printing shop, there is always the Osmond Foundation.

The Osmond Foundation, in which Virl and Tom are joint managers, is a charitable organization designed to encourage research and education in the area of deafness, combat alcoholism and drug abuse, and promote the principle of brotherhood. The hearing losses of Virl and Tom have naturally made them sympathetic to the needs of the deaf generally, and while on their Church missions they were instrumental in setting up a program for the deaf in western Canada. The idea of the Osmond Foundation sprang from their experiences there. It received enthusiastic support from the other family members, and it was in fact the performing group's idea to include alcoholism and drug abuse in the Foundation's concerns, since thousands of letters to their fan club indicated the wide use of these substances among youth.

The performing group not only help with funds but also pitch in on the more mundane tasks such as stuffing envelopes when a mailing goes out. Many people have responded with contributions, and it is a particular concern of the Osmonds and those who guide the funds of the Foundation that the money be directed strictly to the intended purposes. So far as possible too they try to have the funds spent to help people in the particular country or region from which the money was received. ''The beauti-

Virl . . .

Photographer

Production
Manager

ful sounds of this world are taken for granted by most of us," says Virl. "Yet to the deaf, when they first hear, it's as though they have been touched by magic. We are presently working with a unique method for training the deaf to become more aware of sound vibrations."

In the long-term, the aim is to involve fans of the performing group in helping the less fortunate on a personal basis. They can teach the deaf to read; teach deaf children to talk and lip read; or help them to enjoy sports and other active pursuits. "There is such a huge waste of manpower and 'help-power' when kids just do nothing." The energetic Olive almost shudders at the thought. "For example, a lot of them would hang around our apartment in Los Angeles, and this would get themselves and us in trouble with the neighbors and the police and so forth. One day I went out and gave them all a lecture. I said, 'Look at the time you're wasting here! The police won't let the boys come out and talk to you, so it's no good hanging around for that. But why not use your time to help someone. You could go back and find some little handicapped kid who needs time spent on him, needs somebody to talk with him, needs to be loved, needs to be wanted. There's somebody right in your own neighborhood who needs you. Now you go home and find them.' And they did. They got interested in the Foundation in that way; and now we've got many volunteers in that area."

The volunteers are being helped to help others. It all began with the first two Osmond brothers. Virl and Tom feel that the deaf can rise above their handicap. They work to help others along the road they've traveled. That's the kind of brotherhood they and the Osmond Foundation are all about.

18   *What It's All About*

By the time his mother found Brad's note it was too late. Her twenty-year-old son was dead at the end of the yard, a gunshot hole in his head. The note left in his room read:

"Dear Mother and Dad:

I'm sorry, but I just can't go on any longer. The world is crazy. Every day it gets worse — war, suffering, hatred, corruption, greed, frustration, confusion. I'm not getting anywhere — with school, with Sue, with anything. There's no meaning to life and it's not worth the struggle.

Thanks for everything,
Brad"

An extreme case, perhaps, but a common one, a situation which in its essential features is repeated by the thousands annually across the United States and in many other lands. Nor does youth have a monopoly on suicide; it makes an equal appeal to older folk. It can be a response to stress, fear, feelings of insecurity, incurable illness, general despair. Yet it is evident that many people surmount such difficulties and survive. Some do more than this and go on to live fruitful lives. Aside from those who commit the act under the impulsion of a deranged mind, what causes some to succumb and some to surmount?

Camera-span of a family home evening takes in four generations

Family outing takes in warm sunshine and cool drink

Sunday at home – on the way to church

Sunday on tour – George introduces a family presentation
to a local congregation

Of the possible answers, Brad's note perhaps puts the finger on the key, a phrase of enormous significance to everyone — "meaning to life." If a person sees life as an endless maze of restricted and basically insignificant choices or as a limitless plain leading nowhere, his responses to life and its problems and opportunities are likely to be on the negative side. Conversely the concept of an uplifting purpose in life should call forth positive responses.

What has all this to do with the Osmonds? Plenty. The distinguishing mark of this family and the basic motivation of their lives is their concept that life has deep meaning — a meaning which prompts them not merely to survive, to exist, but to truly live.

"Our album 'The Plan' reflects the philosophy we have on this," says Alan, "though we couldn't spell out all the detail there. For a start, basically we believe that all people lived in another sphere in spirit form before we came to this earth in physical bodies, and that we'll all live again in a physical form at some time after this earth life is over — that there is no end to each individual's existence."

Ah! Reincarnation! Not so, says Wayne. "I was explaining my beliefs once to someone I met on a plane, and he made the same comment, but as I understand it, reincarnation has a person appearing in several different physical forms, for repeat performances in mortal life. That's not our belief, and it's certainly not scriptural. Each individual gets only one chance at mortal life. We knew this as spirits before we came here (though all memory of that former life has been temporarily erased) and we knew too that this life would be a testing ground, that our ultimate level of existence would depend upon the level we chose to live here, the kind of principles we learned to live by."

How did this plan come into being? Marie picks up the question. "There never was a plan without a planner — anyone who builds the simplest thing knows that, and the universe, which is all part of the plan, is far from simple. The plan was made by the Supreme Intelligence, the being Christians know as God."

"He's known too by another name." Like his brothers, Jay will explain this concept to you at the drop of a hat. "We call him Father, Father in heaven. He's actually the father of our spirit bodies, and that makes our relationship with him very personal. He has a body shaped like ours, only it's more glorious. We communicate with him through prayer. He loves us all, every one of the billions of his children. He's kind, but like an earthly father (though in a perfect way, of course, because he's perfect) he sometimes has to discipline us."

What is this being doing all the time? "He's managing his creations," says Merrill, "and probably bringing other worlds into being. Scientists now admit the likelihood of intelligent life existing in myriads of other solar systems besides our own. I believe this is so, and that God is the architect of all those worlds too, all inhabited by beings like us, his spirit children. His plan is the same for all these people — to help them reach the highest ultimate level of existence, that is, life on the same level as his. Everyone in this world is a long way from that level now, but the time span is vast, and the possibility and the means are there for those who choose to make the effort. Many of course won't do so."

That is another major point in the Osmond concept of life's purpose, the matter of choice. They believe that God has given man agency, the right and the power to choose for himself; that no one forces us to do good or evil and there's no fate or destiny that awaits anyone regardless

The septet relax outdoors

Not too unrelaxed indoors in family
planning session (Virl's wife Chris at extreme right)

of what he does. "Every man's fate is himself," as one thinker put it. This explains much of the injustice and suffering in the world, since God cannot abrogate man's agency even when he uses it to prey on his fellowmen. But in the great accounting the question will be what each person did with the knowledge and environment he had.

An interesting concept of life. Where did the Osmonds get it all from? "From the scriptures," explains Donny. "Most of it is in the Bible, if you know where to look; and then there are other books we regard as modern scriptures which round out the story. It's an exciting way to view life. Best of all, it's true."

Knowing what makes these Osmonds tick, it's not too difficult to comprehend their reactions. On the negative side they are worlds removed from Brad's solution to life's problems, for they see human life as sacred and the deliberate snuffing out of one's own or another's life as a crime against the Giver of life. Convenience abortion is wrong for similar reasons, whatever modern society and its laws may permit. Sexual immorality ranks high on the list of condemned actions, not only for its long-term effects on the human personality but because it reduces to the level of a lustful, earthy appetite an urge designed to further the highest purposes of the plan of life, the combined urge of true love and procreative power, and which therefore is appropriate only within the bounds of marriage and family life. Drug abuse as well as alcohol, tobacco, and other harmful substances tear down nature's priceless gift of a physical body and at the same time hamper spiritual development, and are thus ruled out by the Osmond philosophy.

On the positive side, Alan offers, "Life is given to us to grow and develop in. It's not primarily for the purpose of making money, for example. Money is a means, not an end, and like our other resources it should be honorably obtained and then used for the growth and benefit of ourselves and others. Character and knowledge are just about the only things we can take with us. It's these things we should develop individually and in the family."

"In the family." That phrase perhaps more than any other epitomizes the Osmond approach, for in their concept the family is an eternal unit, meant to endure forever and not end at death. Over the years this family has already exhibited an unusual degree of "togetherness," not least in the sense of a mutual learning experience. From their earliest years the boys remember a motto inscribed by one of the parents and hung in a prominent position in the various houses they have lived in. It read: "Prepare yourself, and the opportunity will come." By any measure of worldly success the members of this family have met that goal. But for them, larger goals remain. They are still preparing, for in their concept of life, eternity will be studded with opportunities.

Yes, it makes a tremendous difference what one's convictions are about life. "Life has meaning," someone once wrote. "To find that meaning is my meat and drink." The Osmonds have found that meaning, and it tastes good.